KV-029-266

Aldo Lusini · Sandro Chierichetti

Siena

*An illustrated guide book
with the plan of the monuments*

VI edition

Published by Stefano Venturini · Siena

GIOVANNI DI PAOLO: *Paradise* (detail of the *Last Judgement* (1460-1465). Siena, NATIONAL PICTURE GALLERY)

The photos printed in this book were kindly supplied by: Omnia-foto, Turin; Fotocelere, Turin; Angeli, Terni; Grassi, Siena; Venturini, Siena; Cappello, Milano.

Translated by GOOGIE MARAVENTANO

All rights reserved to
Moneta 20127

Contents

★

Siena (62.000 inhabitants) is situated in the very heart of Tuscany at 70 km. from Florence and 231 km. from Rome along the Cassia Way. She is shaped like a huge letter Y lying at 320 metres above sea level on top of three hills overlooking the Arbia and the Elsa valleys. The junction of the three branches of the Y corresponds more or less to « Piazza del Campo ». The northern branch of the Y is called « Terzo di Camollia », the two southern branches « Terzo di Città » and « Terzo di S. Martino ». These three « Terzi » are divided into seventeen districts called « Contrade ». The uneven level of the ground affords suggestive views and most interesting perspectives.

Though old, Siena enjoys all modern comforts; she has good Hotels and restaurants and many little inns called « trattorie » where prices are reasonable. Public offices are efficient and visitors welcome.

About 2 km. from the town on the road to Scacciapensieri, in a very good panoramic position near the « Basilica dell'Osservanza (see page 176), there is a very modern Camping called *Siena-Colleverde* : tel. 20.044.

For reliable information apply to one of the following offices :

ENTE PROVINCIALE PER IL TURISMO (Via di Città, 5).

AZIENDA AUTONOMA DI TURISMO (Palazzo Sansedoni, Banchi di Sotto, 20. Tel. 21.093) which is the seat of the CENTRO TURISTICO DELLA CITTÀ DI SIENA. It has a very good library.

UFFICIO VIAGGI « SETI » (Palazzo Sansedoni, Piazza del Campo, 56. Tel. 23.004 - 41.126 and at the station) for tickets and information.

UFFICIO INFORMAZIONI, PROPAGANDA AND EXCHANGE. (Palazzo Sansedoni, Piazza del Campo, 55. Tel. 20,551 - 21.978).

An accurate visit to Siena, following the five itineraries here described, takes at least one week. Visitors who cannot stay so long should only go to the most important monuments, such as : the CATHEDRAL, page 60 ; the BAPTISTERY, page 97 ; the MUSEO DELL'OPERA METROPOLITANA (the Museum of the Cathedral), page 86 ; the TOWN HALL, page 39 ; the PICTURE GALLERY, page 101 ; the BASILICA OF ST. MARY OF THE SERVI, page 147 ; the BASILICA OF ST. FRANCIS, page 136 ; the BASILICA OF ST. AUGUSTINE, page 124 ; the CHURCH OF S. DOMENICO, page 161 ; the HOUSE OF ST. CATHERINE, page 156 ; CHIGI SARACINI PALACE, page 57 ; the STATE ARCHIVES, page 143.

For the connections with the « Autostrada del Sole » motorway in the North (Florence-Certosa) in the South (Betolla) see the attached plan.

Fig. 1. - Siena - Panorama from San Martino.

Siena

Though art is lavished everywhere in Italy, Siena is still to be considered as one of the richest artistic towns. Each Italian town has a « colour » of its own according to the characteristics of its architectural lines. Rome, for instance — the town which, except for the old classical remnants, belongs to the late Renaissance and Baroque period — represents grandiose majesty and abundance wedded to riches; Venice — the oriental-gothic town — shows us the enchanting beauty of her marbles, colours and arabesques reflected on the water; Florence — the cradle of humanism and of the Renaissance — the studied harmony of form which reveals a very deep inner equilibrium.

The « colour » of Siena lies in her mediaeval austerity softened, as one might say, by a sweet and gentle smile; this particular architecture of hers distinguishes her from her sister towns and at the same time links her to them in art. Should we compare Tuscany to a precious artistic jewel, Siena would appear as one of the brightest gems only to be surpassed in beauty and magnificence by Florence. This gem might well bear the symbolic name of *the Town of the Italian Gothic style*.

What is the meaning of the word « Gothic » according to our point of view? This word is most common in art but acquires a peculiar meaning when applied to Italy. No pure Gothic architectural monuments exist in Italy but there are many monastic buildings which recall the fundamental features of the trans-alpine Gothic art. For instance : very near Siena, the Abbey of San Galgano and inside the town the Church of San Domenico; the cathedral of Milan and many others. Their prevailing feature is verticality and the characteristic element the ogive arch. However, these monuments are but reminders of the fundamental characteristics of the pure Gothic style, so that we should rather speak of « Ogival » art in Italy than of Gothic. This form of art always bears evidence of the influence of other styles, for instance of the Byzantine in Venice and of the Classic-Romanesque in Florence. In Siena the Gothic style is more « Italian » than elsewhere because here the pure Gothic austerity is mitigated by the natural charm and serene smile of our civilization.

Where Siena is essentially Gothic is in the art of painting because her school reached its climax in the lapse of time from the late years of the 13th century to the middle of the 14th. A « happy school belonging to a happy people » it was styled, and with good reason considering that Florentine art, so much more philosophical than the Sienese, though not so poetical, was styled « sad ». In the proper sense, however, Sienese painting was not at all « happy ». All the best masterpieces from Duccio di Buoninsegna to the Lorenzetti brothers stand to prove that is was, instead, pervaded with deep melancholy, at times graceful but certainly never gay. According to the rules of psychology we may say that Sienese painting is sweet and melancholic with marked touches of mysticism. An unshed tear is in the sweet almond shaped eyes of the Sienese Virgins and their parted lips seem to whisper : « I have suffered through You and with You and I show You mercy ».

So, Siena is the town of Gothic art, first of all because her greatest artists lived and worked during the Gothic period, and then for historical reasons as during that period, and particularly under the « Governo dei Nove » (the government of the Nine), the town enjoyed greater prosperity than in any other time.

It is uncertain whether the first inhabitants of Siena were Romans or Gauls though the She-wolf sukling Romulus and Remus, still now the symbol of the town, has often been interpreted as a clear demonstration of her Roman origin. A legend, also, tells us that Ascius and Senius, the sons of Remus, fled from Rome to escape the wrath of their uncle Romulus and that they stopped on their way to offer sacrifices to Diana and Apollo for the happy issue of their enterprise; they called that place Castelsenio. As time went by a town gradually developed around that spot and was called Siena; Castelsenio is now only the name of a district of Siena. The same legend informs us that Senius rode a white horse and Ascius a black one, and this accounts for the fact that these two colours became the symbol of the town (the back and white *Balzana*). Another legend, instead, tells us that during the sacrifices offered by Senius and Ascius to Diana and Apollo, white smoke arose from the altar of the Goddess and black smoke from that of the God.

The Gallic origin of Siena is legendary, too, as it has never been proved that Siena was founded by the *Galli Senones,* or *Senes;* the same must be said about her Etruscan origin. The information we have is based on nothing but supposition but, according to Tacitus and Pliny, most certain is the fact that at a certain moment Siena belonged to Imperial Rome and bore the name of *Sena Julia,* or *Urbs Lupata* because of the She-wolf in her coat-of-arms. The first evangelist seems to have been Ansano Anicio of the noble Roman Anicia family, who died a martyr during the reign of Diocletian in the year 303.

Siena acquired importance in the early Middle Ages; she gained strength during the feudal age and reached the apex of her power during the Communal age. Life in Siena in feudal times was more or less the same as in all the other towns of central and northern Italy.

After the rule of the Lombards from 570 to 770 and that of the Frankish Counts from the 10th century to the 11th the Bishops gained supremacy and Siena reached the apex of her feudal life. Then the feudal system began to fall and its increasing weakness prepared the way to the Communal age which lasted from the 11th century to the 12th. But before the definite rise of the Commune much struggling went on between the Bishops and the people who were represented by three Consuls, two chosen from the laic feudal patricians and one from the merchants of the town. In times to come they originated the bourgeoisie. In 1147 Bishop Raniero was compelled to quit Siena; then the supremacy of the Commune began.

Life during the communal age was extremely complex. At first a policy of expansion both territorial and economical was adopted, but it gradually had to be abandoned for a conservative policy of peace. Inside the town life was hard because the slightest disturbance in the equilibrium either of the social or of the economical forces of the Commune caused fierce struggling, sometimes with the intervention of foreign elements. At first there was a progressive tendency to the supremacy of the richer classes (timocracy), later on to that of the people (democracy), then for quite a long time the two parties were victorious by turns. Frequent were, therefore, conflicts between the nobles themselves, between the nobles and the rich merchants, between the latter and the common people. At times real coalizations of classes were formed : of nobles and proletariats, for instance, to fight against some common enemy and establish a new form of government.

After a period of territorial expansion at the expense of the neighbouring feuds and lords who, by means of taxes and dues, tried to hinder the development of the town, war broke out between Guelphs and Ghibellines. Siena stood for the latter both for economical and political reasons, particularly because Florence - her most powerful rival - was the Guelph stronghold. This rivalship lasted from the early years of the 12th century till 1269 when Siena was defeated at the battle of Colle Val d'Elsa.

In 1235 Siena lost Montepulciano, Montalcino and Poggibonsi. Soon after, the town enjoyed a period of truce most favourable to her development. By the end of the 12th century Sienese bankers such as Malavolti, Piccolomini, Saracini, Tolomei, Buonsignori and Salimbeni were dealing business all over Europe and even in eastern countries, and before the end of the 13th century they had become the favourite bankers of the Papacy.

The wealthy condition of the middle classes (« grassa borghesia » - fat bourgeoisie, as they were called because they were rich) soon affected the political life of the town. Then the « Consoli » (Consuls) were succeeded by a « Podestà » (1199). In 1236 the « Consiglio dei Ventiquattro » (Council of the Twenty-four) was created to represent the people; twelve members were chosen from the common people and twelve from the noble Ghibellines. In 1262 a « Capitano del Popolo » (Captain of the People) was created. The administration of the town was then in the hands of the « Provveditori di Biccherna e di Gabella » with their Magistrate called « Camarlingo » (Magistrato di Biccherna; see page 144).

In 1255 war with Florence broke out again and the Sienese were defeated at Monteriggioni. Then Siena asked the help of King Manfred of Swabia but the Sienese were again defeated by the Florentines at the battle of Monteaperti on September 4th . 1260 (This battle is mentioned in Canto X, v. 86 of Dante's 'Inferno' and also in Canto XXXII, v. 81). After that, Ghibellinism definitely became the leading party in Tuscany but was not of much help to Siena. The town was then devoted to Virgin Mary meaning thus to express the people's gratitude for the protection the Sienese had enjoyed; she was then styled Civitas Virginis.

As a reaction the Papacy no longer borrowed money of the Ghibelline Sienese bankers and the town was excomunicated. In the long run this event proved of extreme importance to Siena; it was the cause of an economical crisis because insolvent debtors enjoyed the protection of the Papacy. A good many of the rich Sienese merchants were then compelled to turn to the Guelphs for protection; in this way politics soon affected economy again but this time in a most unfavourable manner. In the past, while struggling against Florence, the Sienese had turned to Ghibellinism to protect their interests in the commercial field; now, instead, for the same reason they were compelled to turn to the Guelphs.

To make the condition of the Ghibellines still worse, in 1266 King Manfredi died fighting at Benevento and in

1268 Charles of Anjou had Conrad of Swabia beheaded at Tagliacozzo. The Guelphs were still very strong in Florence and enjoyed the help of the French-Anjouine troups. On June 11th. 1269 a battle was fought at Colle Val d'Elsa (the little town that rebelled against Siena); the Sienese were defeated and their Captain Provenzano Salvani, the victorious hero at the battle of Monteaperti, was killed.

These events were a deadly stroke to Ghibellinism. The Guelphs siezed the town and the Ghibellines retired to Arezzo. The governors were deposed (the body called « Consiglio dei Ventiquattro ») and replaced with men chosen among the Guelphs themselves. Many were then the changes in the Government of the town : from 1271 to 1280 a body of thirty-six Guelph Captains ruled; from 1280 to 1286 a body of fifteen Governors and defensors; from 1287 to 1355 a body of Priors and Defensors called « Consiglio dei Nove » (Council of the Nine) or « Noveschi ».

Like it happened with the « Consiglio dei Ventiquattro » (the Council of the Twentyfour) the middle classes then enjoyed supremacy. They were called « popolo grasso » or « borghesia mercantile » (the fat people, or mercantile bourgeoisie). Peace was then established with all the neighbouring towns, and particularly with Florence and much progress was made in the economical civil and artistic fields. On the whole, the middle class government was the best Siena ever had. Nevertheless things grew ever more difficult even for the « Noveschi » after the faillure of a certain bank called « Banca dei Buonsignori » and through the everlasting conflicts between the most powerful Sienese patricians (the Tolomei and the Salimbeni, in particular).

To make things worse in 1326 the town suffered famine and in 1348 there was a terrible plague. The nobles and the lower classes till then excluded from the government of the town then made an alliance to overthrow the « Governo dei Nove ». Helped by Emperor Charles V, at that time Lord of Siena, (he was banished in 1356) they succeeded in their enterprise but a very unsettled state of things ensued. Several forms of government were tried by turns: in 1355 the « Governo dei Dodici di Popolo » (chosen from the middle classes) which lasted till 1368 when other similar forms of government were adopted one after another; the characteristic feature of them all, however, was the supremacy of the working classes. From 1400 to 1405 the Visconti family ruled the town. That was a very dark period indeed brightened only by two great mystics: St. Catherine from 1347 to 1380 and St. Bernardine from 1380 to 1444.

The seigniory of the Visconti was followed by a time in which the supremacy of the lower classes was absolute; the government was called « Governo dei Priori ». Just then Alfonso Duca di Calabria, the leader who had helped the Sienese defeat the Florentines at Poggio Imperiale in 1479, was Lord of Siena and the rich bourgeoisie became once more the ruling class, but in collaboration with the lower classes as it was during the rule of the « Noveschi ». An insurrection ensued and the « Noveschi » were banished from the town. The Sienese merchants then assembled at Staggia (a little village near Siena) from where on July 22nd. 1487 they set out to conquer Siena. They succeeded in capturing the town and were strong enough to impose a new regimen which very soon became oligarchic. It was a government formed by a body called « Balia » whose task was to elect a triumvirate known as the « Triumvirato dei Segreti ». At the head of the merchants in their enterprise was Pandolfo Petrucci who availed himself of his authority to establish a dictatorship. At first his attempt was a faillure and he was exiled but only to be recalled to Siena soon after as Lord of the town. He ruled as an absolute governor from 1502 to 1512.

The seigniory of Pandolfo Petrucci, though strong enough to baffle the plans of Alexander VI, of Cesare Borgia, of the King of France, of the Sforza and of the Florentines, was of no consequence. Fabio and Borghese Petrucci, Pandolfo's sons, were compelled to leave the town and Alessandro Bichi ruled at the head of the « Noveschi » till he was killed in 1525 during an insurrection led by a popular party called « Libertini ». When Pope Clement VII who sympathized with the « Noveschi » learned the bad news he was enraged and sent an army against the town but the « Libertini » were able to defeat the Pope's forces at the battle of Camollia on July 25th. 1526.

By that time the Seigniories in Italy were fighting one another for supremacy all over the country and in Europe war was raging everywhere for the same reason. These events, the hostility of the Pope, of the Medici and their ally the King of France compelled Siena to give up the idea of forming new alliances as any enterprise whatever seemed extremely dangerous.

Under the pretence of making peace between the Sienese nobles and the lower classes Charles V, King of Spain, then sent an army to garrison the town (1531) at the head of which was General Ferrante Gonzaga (later on succeeded by his own vicar Giovanni de Luna). The last Commander was Don Diego Hurtado de Mendoza, in 1547, a wicked, corrupt man who had a fortress built inside the town against the Sienese themselves (1551). The material was provided by demolishing, or lowering, a good many of the old towers of which Siena was so proud. Then the Sienese rebelled; on August 5th 1552 they destroyed the Spanish fortress and expelled the Spaniards from the town. (This event goes under the name of « Cacciata degli Spagnoli »). This was the most glorious insurection in the history of Siena. The power of the old republic, however, was by then towards the end and the last years of freedom witnessed the tyrany of the Spaniards and the greed of the Medici .

In 1553 Montalcino (a little village near Siena) fought bravely against Don Garzia di Toledo (March 27th.) and in 1554 Gian Giacomo de' Medici, Marchese di Marignano was compelled to give up the siege of Siena. During the siege inside the town the whole Sienese people, men and women, young and old, were at arms commanded by Biagio di Montluc the Marshal of the King of France, and Piero Strozzi the Florentine exile. Notwithstanding their courage and good will, the defeat of the Sienese at Scannagallo on August 2nd. 1554 and the difficulties to be faced to organise the defence of the population compelled the Sienese to surrender. On April 17th. 1555 the Republic of Siena closed the book of destiny for ever. Seven hundred Sienese families led by Biagio di Montluc then left the town for Montalcino « *ultima e forte rocca di Siena ed ultima minaccia* » C. Marradi says (the last Sienese stronghold and the last menace). There they organized their resistance under the emblem of the Sienese She-wolf suckling the twins. When peace was signed at Cateau-Cambrésis they had to surrender (July 15th. 1559) and Siena was given to Cosimo de' Medici as a Spanish feud except the so called « Stato dei Presidi » that meant the Sienese ports on the Tyrrhenian coasts which, instead, were annexed to the Vice-royalty of Naples.

While the Medici were rulers Siena flourished. In 1624 the « Monte dei Paschi » was founded, now one of the most important banks of Italy, and in 1656 the traditional Palio was run for the first time. Life was easy even under the House of Lorrain and all through the Napoleonic wars till 1859 when the town was joined to the Mother Country.

ART

By the end of the 13th. century all forms of art were most flourishing but they reached the apex of their splendour in the 14th. century. The Sienese school of paintinè, in particular, deceloped a most refined style of its own quite different to the styles of all the other towns.

ARCHITECTURE. In Tuscany during the 11th and 12th centuries the Romanesque style prevailed everywhere, but particularly in Florence and Pisa. (The Cathedral of Pisa is, in fact, one of the finest Romanesque monuments in Italy). In Siena instead this style was rather rare; few are indeed the pure Romanesque churches in Siena and all of them are faithful to the Lombard models with very few new decorative elements. They are stone buildings decorated with little pensile arches: the Church of San Donato, that of San Cristoforo, of Santa Maria di Betlemme, of San Pietro alla Magione and of Sant'Andrea. The lower part of the facade of the Cathedral built by Giovanni Pisano is, on the whole, Romanesque too, but it shows signs of Gothic influences. Inside, notwithstanding the many styles so admirably blended, the characteristic fundamental features of the Romanesque buildings are plainly visible though mixed up with architectural elements of Lombard origin and with Pisan-Oriental decorations (for instance, the black and white stripes). Like in many other towns of Tuscany also in Siena the prevailing Romanesque element was the tower-like house (see Sant'Ansano and the house of the Forteguerri family).

By the 14th. century the Gothic style was in full splendour in Siena. In 1224 at a place near Siena called San Galgano the Cistercian Monks began an Abbey which took till 1288 to be completed. Though spoilt it still stands as a link between the original French Gothic style and the Tuscan. The verticality and linear perspective of the northern models is mitigated in Siena by the harmony of the classical traditions and the Sienese Gothic is even different to the Florentine; it is not so severe, maybe not so well balanced but far more fanciful and light.

The Cathedral of Siena, still now considered as one of the most complex Italian stylistic problems, was completed just when the Gothic style was at its best. The upper part of the facade is pure Gothic and the whole prospect is far nearer to the Gothic decorative models than to the Romanesque. During the same period the apse was enlarged and the vaults completed over the high altar. The grand *"Duomo Nuovo"* (new cathedral) was started but had to be abandoned owing to a succession of unhappy events. Among the artists who worked at the completion of the Cathedral, and started the new cathedral, worthy of mention are: Tino di Camaino and Camaino di Crescentino, Lando di Pietro, Giovanni di Agostino, Domenico di Agostino and Giovanni di Cecco.

The facade of the Baptistery was also built during the Gothic age and so were the Churches of San Francesco, San Domenico, and Santa Maria dei Servi. Simple and severe, decorated with terracotta elements, all these buildings show Lombard reminiscences; they have a single nave and bare beams supporting the roof.

Gothic art prevailed even in the architecture of private houses to such an extent that it determined the very aspect of Siena. The delightful gothic houses with their graceful stylistic decorations, threefold windows and grandiose portals, the monumental patrician mansions and the splendid *"Palazzo Pubblico"* (Town Hall) are, in fact, samples of the essential architectural elements prevailing in Siena. The *"Palazzo Pubblico"* is one of the best in Tuscany; an insuperable model built in the lapse of time from 1288 to 1309. It is a brick building on a stone basement with rows of elegant threefold windows. Many other palaces are decorated after the same style, such as: Palazzo Sansedoni, Palazzo Chigi Saracini, Palazzo Buonsignori and Palazzo Piccolomini Clementini. Other more independent buildings show refined and most original decorative elements (see for instance the Palazzo del Capitano).

The gates of the town are also worthy of attention. They are: Porta Camollia, Porta Romana, Porta San Viene, Porta San Marco and Porta Ovile. The elegant founts are: Fontebranda, Fonte Nuova, Fonte d'Ovile, Fonte di Follonica and Fonte di Pescaia.

The building called « Loggia della Mercanzia » (the merchants' loggia) stands as a link between the Gothic style and the Italian Rinascimento. (The full arches are still a pure Gothic element). During the early years of the Italian Rinascimento Sienese architecture showed Florentine influences chiefly in the works carried out by Bernardo Gamberelli nick-named Rossellino (see Palazzo Piccolomini) and by Giuliano da Maiano (see Palazzo Spannocchi). The building called « Loggia del Papa » and the mansion known as « Palazzo dei Diavoli » with the adjoining church are instead the work of a Sienese artist called Antonio Federighi, from 1444 to 1490. Many buildings of minor importance show the influence of this art. Another Sienese architect who deserves mention (above all in the military field) is Francesco di Giorgio Martini (1439-1502) but the greatest of them all, the glory of the Rinascimento was Baldassarre Peruzzi (1481-1536). However, his best works are in Rome; in Siena he built Palazzo Pollini, once Celsi, and left many pupils and imitators.

The Baroque period is represented in Siena by the beautiful Basilica of Santa Maria di Provenzano built by Flaminio del Turco to Domenico Schifardini's order, and by some fine buildings due to Giovanni Fontana. During the 18th. century the facade of the old Church of San

Giorgio and that of the Church of San Vigilio were completed by Giovanni Pietro Cremoni.

SCULPTURE. The first sculptors who worked in Siena came from Pisa during the Romanesque period; they were Nicola Pisano and his son Giovanni with a group of collaborators. Nicola produced the pulpit in the Cathedral, a masterpiece only to be compared to the pulpit formerly sculptured by the same artist for the Baptistery in Pisa, He worked in Siena as a sculptor and as an architect during the last years of the 13th. century to complete the lower part of the facade of the Cathedral. He is the first and most important representative of the Sienese Gothic sculpture. His statues on the facade of the Cathedral were the models to which his followers turned for inspiration and teaching, though none of them ever reached the master's dramatic pathos and expression, not even Tino di Camaino, the best of them all, whose works show great stylistic mastery (plasticism prevails in his groups). Other followers of Giovanni Pisano's are Giovanni di Agostino, Goro di Gregorio, Gano and Lorenzo Maitani (these two artists never worked in Siena), and Ramo di Paganello who worked also at Orvieto to complete the facade of that lovely Cathedral.

After a parenthesis which lasted all through the late years of the 14th. century Jacopo della Quercia made Sienese sculpture famous (1372-1438). This artist might be styled the spiritual son of Nicola Pisano. Just when the Italian Rinascimento was dawning he entirely renewed Sienese art by carrying it back to the poetical forms of life so rich in moral and religious values. In Siena Jacopo della Quercia produced the fountain called « Fonte Gaia » (the Gay Fountain). With some of his collaborators he next produced the splendid baptismal Font, later on decorated with basreliefs by Ghiberti and Donatello. This piece of sculpture is an admirable compendium of Tuscan art.

Among Jacopo della Quercia's disciples the worthiest are Pietro del Minella, Giovanni di Treno, Goro di Neroccio and Antonio Federighi.

Soon after Ghiberti and Donatello came Urbano da Cortona and Lorenzo di Pietro nicknamed Vecchietta

(1412-1480). Vecchietta was the clever continuator of Donatello's art who influenced Francesco di Giorgio Martini the worthy master, and his disciple Giacomo Cozzarelli the delightful carver (1453-1515).

Clever at Antonio Federighi's kind of decorative art was Giovanni di Stefano nicknamed Sassetta whose mastery was equalled by another great artist: Lorenzo di Mariano nicknamed Marrina (1476-1534). We are by now at the middle of the 16th. century; the later years saw Domenico Beccafumi's bronze statues and Fulvio Signorini's marble groups (1486-1551 the former, ...1591-1609 the latter). Then Sienese sculpture became silent. The Baroque period and even the period that followed it did not contribute any important names. The only works worthy of mention in those long barren years are those produced by Dionisio Mazzuoli and his sons Giuseppe (1644-1725) and Giovanni Antonio with the collaboration of a nephew of theirs called Bartolomeo; however they were but clever imitators of Bernini's style. In the 19th. century two gliorious names appeared: Giovanni Duprè (1817-1882) and Tito Sarrocchi (1824-1890). Last came Emilio Gallori (1854-1924) and Patrizio Fracassi (1875-1903).

PAINTING. The glory of Siena is, indeed, her school of painting. From the 13th. century to the 15th. over four hundred painters contributed exquisite works of art to the patrimony of the town.

The very early works of the Sienese school show the influence of Romanesque and Byzantine art. To this period belongs Guido da Siena's famous Madonna which bears his signature and the date 1221; now it is treasured in the « Palazzo Pubblico » (Town Hall).

The father of the Sienese school of painting is Duccio di Buoninsegna (...1260-1319). At first he only produced minatures but he soon turned to painting. His personality was such that his works were real models of all the fundamental characteristics of the Sienese school for a period that lasted over one hundred years. In consideration of this we may say that his large picture called « Maestà » (now in the Museum of the Cathedral) besides being one of the most amazing masterpieces of Italian art is the very « key » of the values of the Sienese school in particular.

In early times Sienese painting was under the influence of Byzantine art; it was a fanciful kind of painting as the allegorical values were, in general, preferred to the narrative and symbolism prevailed over reality. The drawing was felt not only as a simple decorative element but as a highly expressive factor, and colour as the main feature of painting. The Gothic style was therefore the most congenial to the spirit of the Sienese school.

Besides the above mentioned picture called « Maestà » very few of Duccio's works are now in Siena but a large crowd of his pupils and followers dwelt inside the town to carry on his teachings; the best were Ugolino di Nerio and Segna di Bonaventura.

Soon after Duccio the imperishable glory of the Sienese school was brightened by Simone Martini, the friend of Petrarca (1283-1344) who linked the Byzantine traditions to the Gothic style thus giving rise to a form of art which reached the highest stylistic values. The few traces of Romanesque art still visible in Duccio's works are no longer to be found in Simone Martini's; the figures this artist painted are sad but sweet and melodious.

Two other names on which rests the glory of the Sienese school are those of the Lorenzetti brothers; Pietro (1280-1348?) is the nearer to the spirit of Duccio di Buoninsegna and of Simone Martini though he gives greater importance to the dramatic values of human psychology and of human forms. Ambrogio Lorenzetti (... 1318-1348) is the more complex of the two brothers; though faithful to the Sienese traditions he is very near to the plastic and spacial values of the Florentine ideals.

From Simone Martini and his brother-in-law Lippo Memmi (... 1317-1356) and, further back in time, from Duccio di Buoninsegna and the Lorenzetti brothers (Pietro in particular) descended a very numerous crowd of artists who contributed much to Sienese art and created an eclectic style of their own. The best worked during the later half of the 14th. century following no particular model but keeping very near to Simone Martini's style. The worthiest were: Barna (... 1340-1381) who drew inspiration from Duccio and Simone Martini. Bartolo di Fredi

(1330-1410) a follower of Simone Martini's and of the Lorenzetti brothers. Taddeo di Bartolo (1363-1422). Niccolò di Ser Sozzo Tegliacci (...1334-1363), Naddo Ceccarelli, Lucca di Tommè, Jacopo di Mino del Pellicciaio, Paolo di Neri, Lippo Vanni, Andrea Vanni the disciple of St. Catherine, Andrea di Bartolo and Paolo di Giovanni Fei.

At the beginning of the 15th. century even in Siena prevailed a style called « international style » the characteristic of which was the return to the elegant Gothic decorative values. Two great artists then appeared; Stefano di Giovanni nicknamed Sassetta (1392-1450) and Giovanni di Paolo (1399?-1482). They may be classified among the brightest names of the Italian Trecento because in Siena the new « international style » was but the continuation of the Gothic traditions. Sassetta's works are dreamy fabuluos and sweet; bewitching and extremely lyrical are those of Giovanni di Paolo, the exquisite decorator who might well be compared to the Oriental artists. From 1400 to 1447 worked Domenico di Bartolo whose mastery is undeniable; this artist was influenced by the art of Masaccio. The art of Lorenzo di Pietro nicknamed Vecchietta, often mentioned as a sculptor, is of Florentine derivation and shows reminiscences of the art of Sassetta. Next to him come Matteo di Giovanni (1430?-1495) the greatest Sienese master of the late Quattrocento, and Francesco di Giorgio Martini (1439-1502) the eclectic architect, sculptor and painter whose works, however, are within the limits of the Sienese traditions. Guidoccio Cozzarelli (... 1450-1516) painted some beautiful Madonne after the style of Matteo di Giovanni, and so did Neroccio di Bartolomeo Landi (1447-1500) though his style was rather independent.

These were the last clever artists of the Sienese school for quite a long period of time. The models of the Tuscan School and of the Umbrian were then imitated and repeated over and over again till they lost their originality and vigour. Pollaiolo and Botticelli, both Tuscan, are however to be praised together with Pinturicchio, the Umbrian master, who frescoed the walls of the « Libreria Piccolomini » in the Cathedral.

During the early years of the 16th. century Giovanni Antonio Bazzi nicknamed Sodoma contributed much to painting in Siena though he was born at Vercelli in 1477. He was a clever artist faithful to Leonardo da Vinci's style. He soon became the master to whom a large number of followers turned for inspiration. His cleverest pupil was Domenico Beccafumi nicknamed Mecarino (1486-1551) whose stricking personality soon won him fame. He assimilated the art of Michelangelo, Raffaello and Fra Bartolomeo as well as Sodoma's style; his dramatic power was remarkable, his chiaro-scuro perfect and the vast range of his chromatic tones almost exceptional. He produced all the best drawings for the stories engraved on the floor of the Cathedral.

Other artists who turned to Sodoma for inspiration are: Baldassarre Peruzzi, the worthy architect whose paintings remind us of Pinturicchio, Raffaello and Michelangelo, and Brescianino who reminds us of Sodoma and Raffaello and other minor Tuscan painters.

As the century drew towards the end the art of painting became even more silent. The only artists to be mentioned are: Arcangelo Salimbeni (1530?-1580?) and a few of his followers, and Rutilio Manetti (1571-1639) who was influenced by Caravaggio.

The art of the 18th. century was conventional and finical. The artists were above all decorators and nothing more. The best was; Giuseppe Nasini (1664-1736).

The best representatives of the art of the 19th. century are: Cesare Maccari (1840-1919), Alessandro Franchi (1838-1914) and Amos Cassioli (1832-1891).

MINOR ARTS. All the Sienese artists of the past excelled in those works of art which required not only skill but precision, constancy and a very refined decorative taste.

Marble Engravings. The floor of the Cathedral of Siena is a most eloquent witness of the skill of the artists of the past in drawing scenes for their stories, and also of that of all the humble carvers who carved the pieces of different coloured marble. These carvers were called « spianatori ».

Wood Carving. The masterpieces of Sienese art in this field are the following: the chancel in the Cathedral, drawn by Francesco del Tonghio (1300?-1388?) of which now only the lateral parts exist; the Chapel in the « Palazzo Pubblico » (Town Hall) produced by Niccolò de' Cori (1363 1453?); one of the choristers' galleries in the Cathedral and a wooden chest in the Palazzo Pubblico; the Choir of the Collegiata di San Quirico produced by Antonio Barili (1453-1516?); the ceiling of the Oratory of San Bernardino in Siena, by Ventura di Ser Giuliano Turapilli (1470?-1522) and the organ of the Basilica dell'Osservanza near Siena made by G.B. Panichi. Most of the precious Sienese wood carvings are in other towns.

Jewellery. This art flourished in Siena from the 12th. century to the 15th. The Sienese goldsmiths, in fact, were famous at that time all over Europe and particularly in England. The best masterpieces of this kind are: A reliquary « *Reliquario del Corporale* » made in 1338 by the Sienese Ugolino di Vieri for the Cathedral of Orvieto; the « *Reliquario della testa di San Galgano* » made on purpose for the head of San Galgano during the 13th. century, now in the « Metropolitana Museum » in Siena. It was ascribed to Lando di Pietro the famous Sienese goldsmith of the 14th. century. During the 15th. century the most remarkable goldsmiths were Bartolomeo di Tommè, Viva di Lando, Toro di Petruccio, Goro di Neroccio and Francesco d'Antonio.

Miniatures. Exquisite miniatures were produced by all the best Sienese artists, such as, for instance, Duccio di Buoninsegna, Ambrogio and Pietro Lorenzetti, Simone Martini, Sano di Pietro, Lippo Vanni, Giovanni di Paolo, Matteo di Giovanni, Benvenuto di Giovanni and Guidoccio Cozzarelli but the worthiest masters in this field were Maestro del Codice di San Giorgio and Niccolò di Ser Sozzo Tegliacci. The best specimen of this art are now treasured in the Piccolomini Library inside the Cathedral, in the State Archives and in the Communal Library called the « Intronati ».

Stained Glass. The Sienese artist who excelled in this art is Pastorino de' Pastorini (1508-1592). The rose window in the apse of the Cathedral is one of the very first stained glasses produced in Italy very likely by the Sienese painters Dono and Giunta di Paolo to Duccio di Buoninsegna's designs.

— 25 —

In times of old Siena devoted herself to Virgin Mary. This little town had such a rich spiritual life that she might well be styled « Patria di anime » (land of souls). An endless crowd of mystics were born in Siena, though a good many of her citizens were reckless and dissipated. This spiritual contrast might be interpreted as the confirmation of the allegory of the contrasting colours of the « Balzana » (the black and white symbol of the town). Religion and mysticism contributed much to the originality of Sienese art.

The first Sienese anchorets and penitents lived in the 9th. century. Their dwelling was an underground corridor over which in later years was built the hospital called « Spedale di Santa Maria della Scala » founded by a cobbler called Sorore.

Many were the mystics who dwelt and preached in Siena in all times; the most important are: in the 13th. century, Ambrogio Sansedoni, Andrea Gallerani, Pietro Pettinaio the first Franciscan Tertiary, Bernardo Tolomei the founder of the Monastery of Monteoliveto Maggiore. The 14th. century saw Pietro Petroni the founder of the Certosa di Maggiano, Giovanni Colombini the founder of the Gesuati, Filippo degli Agazzari and Caterina Benincasa (St. Catherine of Siena). The glorious name of the 15th. century was Bernardino Albizzeschi (St. Bernardine of Siena). The 16th. century saw Bartolomeo Carosi nicknamed Brandano the Madman of Christ, Margherita Bichi, Caterina Vannini who corresponded with Cardinal Federico Borromeo. Passitea Crogi belongs to the 17th. century and David Lazzaretti the prophet of Mount Amiata to the 19th. He closes the list of the Sienese mystics.

CULTURE

Many traditional Academies still stand to prove the antiquity and continuity of Sienese culture and dialectics. Besides the glorious names pertaining to mystic literature (see for instance St. Catherine's letters, Giovanni Colombini's works, Fra Filippo degli Agazzari's

Fig. 2. - Siena - Panorama from San Prospero.

and St. Bernardine's) the Sienese excelled in all times in all the fields of human activity and thought.

Here is a list of the worthiest citizens: POETS - Folcacchiero dei Folcacchieri in the 12th. century; Cecco Angiolieri who polemized with Dante Alighieri, and Bindo Bonichi in the 13th. century; Simone Serdini in the 14th. century; Ludovico Sergardi known as Quinto Settano, and Bernardino Perfetti in the 15th. century. PROSE WRITERS (stories and tales) - in the 15th. century Gentile Sermini from whose works Shakespeare is supposed to have drawn inspiration for his *Romeo and Juliet*. In the 16th. century Pietro Fortini. HISTORIAS AND DIARISTS - Andrea Dei in the 14th. century; Sigismondo Tizio in the 15th., Orlando Malavolti, Giugurta Tommasi and Alessandro Sozzini in the 16th. century. Giovanni Antonio Pecci in the 18th. century. MEN OF LETTERS AND POLIGRAPHS - Alessandro Piccolomini, Claudio Tolomei, Alessandro Turamini; Girolamo and Scipione Bargagli in the 16th. century; Celso Cittadini in the 17th. century; Girolamo Gigli the author of the « *Vocabolario Cateriniano* » in defence of the Sienese idiom against the Florentine, Uberto Benvoglienti and Isidoro Urgurgieri in the 18th. century; Ettore Romagnoli in the 19th. century. SCIENTISTS - Andrea Mattioli the botanist; Pirro Maria Gabbrielli the naturalist, both in the 17th. century Sallustio Bandini the founder of the science of economy, and Paolo Mascagni the anatomist in the 18th. century; Giuseppe Caselli the inventor of the panthelegraph in the 19th. century. REFORMES - Lelio and Fausto Socini the founders of the school of « Socianism » in Poland, now known as Unitarism; Bernardino Ochino, all in the 16th. century. To modern times belong the names of Federigo Tozzi the novelist (1888-1920) and of Dina Ferri the Sienese shepherdess who wrote exquiste poetry (1908-1930).

Now let us go wandering through the streets of Siena listening to the sweet language of her people, let us admire the solemn palaces with their smiling threefold windows and enter their portals and pass under the arches spanning the lanes that witnessed the life of the Middle Ages. Let us allow these visions to carry us back for a moment to the past and stay a while to admire the lovely Cathedral and the even more delightful Piazza del Campo where twice a year the Sienese relive the passions of the bygone days during the *Palio delle Contrade*.

Itinerary I

PIAZZA DEL CAMPO AND ITS MONUMENTS
[The *Palio* - Fonte Gaia (the Gay Fountain) -
Palazzo Sansedoni - Palazzo Pubblico (Town
Hall)].

THE CAMPO SQUARE
(Piazza del Campo)

Piazza del Campo, often simply called *"il Campo"* is
the historical and topographic centre of the town. It is
one of the most characteristic and scenographic squares
in Italy and dates back to the fruitful days of the Middle
Ages when the Communes prevailed.

The uneven level of the ground on which it is built
(right at the junction of the three hills on top of which
lies Siena) accounts for the fact that it is shaped like
a shell; man, here, availed himself of nature for the
sake of art. Even the way it is paved reminds one of a
shell : in 1347 it was divided into nine brick-paved sections by long radiating stone strips which stood for the government of the « Nine ». On the base of the shell stands
the massive Palazzo Pubblico (Town Hall) whilst the
fan like part is delimited by old battlemented and turreted houses.

All the most important public events in the history
of Siena took place in this square; here the factions
fought against one another and then made peace; here
the Sienese people awaited in prayer to learn the news
of the battle of Monteaperti won by Provenzano Salvani, the Sienese Captain, against the Florentines on
September 4th. 1260; here Provenzano himself went
begging for alms to rescue a friend from the hands
of the enemies who kept him a prisoner (*si ridusse a
tremar per ogni vena* : Dante, *Purg.* XI, vv. 121-138);

Fig. 3 - The *Palio* horse race in the « Campo » square (a picture by **Vittorio Giunti**)

here the inspiring words of Pier Pettinaio, of Fra Filippo degli Agazzari and of St. Bernardine resounded and the people of Siena lived the last days of the siege laid by Charles V at the time of the fall of the Republic (1555).

THE PALIO
(Il Palio)

The *Campo* is still now used for the well known *Palio* horse race (see fig. 3) which is one of the best Italian popular manifestations. It takes place every year on July 2nd. and August 16th. On July 2nd. the Palio is run to celebrate the miraculous apparition of Virgin Mary near the old houses that belonged to Provenzano Salvani. The holy apparition was therefore called « Madonna di Provenzano » in whose honour the very first Palio was run in 1656. On August 16th. the Palio was run the first time in 1701 in honour of the « Madonna dell'Assunta » the patroness and *Advocate* of Siena through all the tragic events since She protected the Sienese militia at the famous battle of Monteaperti against the Florentines.

The *Palio* is a secular historical tradition strictly connected with the origin of the *Contrade of Siena* (districts into which the town is divided). The *Contrade* are agonistic spectacular institutions having each a seat, an oratory a coat of arms, appellations, titles of nobility, emblems and colours, official representatives, festivities, patron Saints, protectors, their own delimited territories and their own population which consists of all those people who were born or live within the topographic limits of the district, according to the proclamation issued by Violante Beatrice of Bavaria on January 7th. 1730, at that time Governess of the town.

Originally the « Contrade » were fifty-nine, at least so it seems; now only seventeen exist ten of which take part in the historical pageant and in the race at each Palio (seven by right and three drawn by lots).

Here is a list of their names, emblems and colours grouped into « Terzi », or « Terzieri » (in olden times the town was divided into three sections called : « Terziere di Città », « Terziere di San Martino » and « Terziere di Camollia »).

Terziere di Città

AQUILA (Eagle) : a double headed eagle with imperial symbols. Colours : yellow with black and blue bands.

CHIOCCIOLA (Snail) : a snail. Yellow and red with blue bands.

ONDA (Wave) : a swimming dolphin wearing a crown. White and blue.

PANTERA (Panther) : a rampant panther. Red and blue with white bands.

SELVA (Forest) : a rhinoceros bearing a huge tree hung with hunting implements. Green and orange-yellow with white bands.

TARTUCA (Tortoise) : a tortoise. Yellow and blue.

Terziere di San Martino

CIVETTA (Owl) : an owl. Colours : black and red with white bands.

LEOCORNO (Unicorn) : a unicorn. White and orange-yellow with blue bands.

NICCHIO (Shell) : a sea-shell (« Nicchio » means sea-shell). Blue with yellow and red bands.

TORRE (Tower) : an elephant with a tower on its back. Dark red with white and blue bands.

VALDIMONTE (Ram) : a rampant ram. White and yellow with red bands.

Terziere di Camollia

BRUCO (Caterpillar) : a caterpillar. Colours : Yellow and green with blue bands.

DRAGO (Dragon) : a flying dragon. Red and green with yellow bands.

GIRAFFA (Giraffe) : a Giraffe. White and red.

ISTRICE (Porcupine) : a porcupine. White, red, black and blue bands.

LUPA (She-Wolf) : the Roman She-Wolf suckling the twins. Black and white with orange-yellow bands.

OCA (Goose) : a crowned goose with the cross of Savoia round its neck. White and green with red bands.

The « Contrade » first appeared at the middle of the 15th. century to celebrate certain solemn events. They were represented by special wooden devices shaped like animals — such as, for instance, a giraffe a dragon, a porcupine,

Fig. 4 - *The Palio* - From top to bottom, left corner: *the « Duce »
of one of the Contrade.* Right corner: *the charriot with the banner
called « drappellone del Palio ».* Left corner: *rejoyeings for the happy
victory.* Right corner: *the representatives of one of the Contrade.*

a she-wolf, a caterpillar, a goose etc. — worked from inside by the youngsters of the districts they represented. They were called after the animals themselves.

Very soon these associations began to organize shows of their own, such as : *bull hunting* (suppressed in 1590), *buffalo races* (only till 1650), donkey races and a game called « Giuoco delle Pugna ».

Precedingly (besides the usual horse-races which took place in many towns of Italy to celebrated certain particular religious and civil events) the Sienese played other kinds of games, such as : *Mazzascudo* (mace and shield) because the players bore maces and shields ; the *Giorgiani* in honour of San Giorgio (battles with blunt weapons) ; *Elmora detto dei cestarelli* because the players wore certain funny baskets (cestarelli) on their heads ; *le Pugna* (punching) abolished in 1324 because the players started throwing stones at one another, then weapons and sticks were used and a real battle ensued. To re-establish order the Bishop was compelled to descend into the square with a train of priests and monks) ; *il Pallone,* a game played between the « Terzi » of the town. A hunge ball was thrown from the top of the « Mangia » tower by the youngsters of one of the « Terzi » into the field of their opponents. This game was played on January 13th. 1555 for Biagio di Montluc the French Marshal.

Of all these games only the *Palio* has survived. The preparations for this parade are slow and methodic like a liturgical procedure. Four days before the day of the Palio trials take place in the « Campo » square which is turned into a racing track. A thick layer of earth is spread on the ground and a row of mattresses is placed against the walls at the dangerous corner of San Martino to protect the jokeys in case they fall.

The whole square is amazingly fit for such kind of manifestations because its shape is that of a mediaeval Roman amphitheatre closed at the base by the straight line of the Palazzo Pubblico. Besides being semicircular this peculiar square is also funnel-shaped like the theatres of the imperial age. Eleven streets run into it though it is extremely difficult to percieve them from the middle of the square. All around the track, perched up against the walls of the houses, seats are ranged one behind and above the other. Windows, balconies and loggias, too, are made ready for the visitors ; 33,000 seats in all, but they are far from sufficient and are always sold out long before the day of the performance. In the centre of the square there is room for about 28.000 people to stand, but this is not enough either and the roofs, the battlements and the cornices of the old houses looking on to the square are also crowded. There are people everywhere, even in the most unlikely places.

On both the appointed days every year the « *Contrade* » — that is to say all the Sienese population — compete for a prize which is but a hand painted silk banner (*pallium*). Each « Contrada » is represented by a group of young men called *Comparsa* ranged as follows: one *drummer*, two *flag-bearers*, with their flags, one « *Duce* » or *captain*, two *grooms*, one *page* carrying a flag with two *pages* at his sides carrying the emblems of the « Contrada », the race-horse called *barbero* with a jockey called *barbaresco*, last the *jokey* who is to run the race on a parade horse called *soprallasso* followed by a *groom* (see fig. 4 and fig. 5-6).

The historical parade is a lively display of rich mediaeval costumes which date back to the period of time from 1430 to 1480; their colours are as bright as one may fancy. The procession goes wending its way round the « Campo » square in the following order: the *flag-bearer of the Commune* on horseback bearing the standard of Siena (the black and white *Balzana*) followed by his *groom*, a group of *macers*, a group of trumpeters and *musicians* called *musici di Pa-*

Fig. 5-6 - Representatives of the *Contrade* at the *Palio*.

lazzo playing on their bugles the march composed for the Palio by Pietro Formichi in 1875, the *Captains*, the *representatives of the « Podestà »* (called *podesterie*), the *standard-bearers* with the standards of the « Terzieri » of the town and of the lands belonging to the Commune called « Masse », the *flag-bearers* of the Corporations of Art, the *captain of the people* (Capitano del popolo) on horseback and a group of flag-bearers with the flags of the old Republic. Next come the representatives of the « *Contrade* » called *comparse* (see fig. 4). The first ten are those which are to run the palio horse race; they are followed by a row of young *pages* bearing festoons of laurel leaves and then by the seven « Contrade » that do not run (they have no « *barbaro* » and no jockey). Next comes the *captain of Justice* (Capitano di Giustizia) riding a horse and then the representatives of the seven « Contrade » that no longer exist : Cock, Lion, Bear, Oak, Sword, Viper. Last comes the triumphal *chariot* (carroccio; see fig. 4) drawn by huge oxen. In the chariot are seated the four *Provveditori di Biccherna* (administrative authority) who in times of yore used to superintend public representations, the oriflamme of the Commune and the *Palio* to be awarded to the victor, and a group of trumpeters.

When this magnificent pageant has slowly gone round the square all the representatives go to sit on a platform raised for the purpose just beneath the windows of the Palazzo Pubblico. When they are all seated there they look like a strange army after some most brilliant victory, or a train of heroes or of poets ready to enter Paradise. As soon as everything is quiet the flag-bearers of all the « Contrade » perform together a game with their flags called « gioco delle bandiere ». They throw them high up into the air and catch them again before they thouch the ground; it is a splendid, most decorative display of colours accompanied with the beating of drums, the sound of bugles and trumpets and the chimes of the big bell on top of the « Mangia » tower; the little bell on the chariot known in Siena as « Martinella » is also very active.

All this is but a prelude, a time of anxiety and expectation. When at last the horses appear and the race starts the crowd becomes delirious. Three times the jockeys goad their horses round the square and the people shout as if the town were about to fall.

The spirit of Siena is in the very colours of her « *Contrade* » and in all the manifestations connected with each of them, first of all the benediction of the horses and jockeys each in the church of their own « *Contrada* » early in the afternoon just before the Palio. It is this spirit that animates the whole manifestation and contributes such enthusiasm and pathos to the scene as may only be found in the Spanish bull-fights.

This traditional popular manifestation lasts four days (from the 29th. of June to the 2nd. of July and from the 13th. to the 16th. of August) and finishes in the streets of the victorious « Contrada » where the people celebrate the happy event in a most joyous way.

Whoever happens to be at Siena during those exciting days can but join the enthusiasm of the people for the *Palio* and, of course, the final victory. Visitors in fact, often go roaming through the winding streets of the old town sympathizing with the *Contrada* in which they are living; they do their best to understand the alliances and rivalries between the *Contrade* and temporarily become fervent *contradaioli* (as the inhabitants of each *Contrada* are called) having much at heart the health of the race horse and of the jockey.

MONUMENTS

Let us walk round Piazza del Campo. First of all let us stop on the left side, facing the Town Hall near the corner of Via Rinaldini (where PALAZZO CHIGI ZONDADARI stands, of old date but repaired by Antonio Valeri in 1824). From here the sloping ground is clearly visible as well as the shell shape of the « Campo ». The Town Hall with the « Mangia » tower is stupendous with its back-ground of imposing buildings; the splendid PALAZZO D'ELCI (14th. century), the zebra-striped belfry of the Cathedral and the cupola stand out in black and white against the predominant brick-red tones of the other houses. Now let us examine the palaces facing the Town Hall.

Almost at the centre of the « Campo » on the highest spot is FONTE GAIA, the Gay Fountain. It was placed there in 1409-1419 and was so called because of the public rejoicings that took place to celebrate its completion. In olden times it was supplied with water by an acqueduct 25 km. long (1343). It was decorated with Jacopo della Quercia's splendid bas-reliefs which, in 1868, were replaced with good reproductions by the Sienese sculptor Tito Sarrocchi (fig. 7). The original remnants are still to be admired in the Loggia of the Town Hall. The actual bas-reliefs from left to right represent: the *Creation of Adam, Wisdom, Hope, Fortitude, Prudence, Virgin Mary with the Holy Child seated between two Angels, Justice, Charity, Temperance, Faith* and the *Expulsion of Adam and Eve from Earthly Paradise.*

From here the whole facade of the Palazzo Pubblico (Town Hall) can be fully admired. On the opposite side from where we started (near the Costarella dei Barbieri) a complete view of all the palaces facing the Town Hall may be enjoyed. Above them all rises the lovely massive PALAZZO SANSEDONI with ist dull red brick facade enlivened with the brighter tones of the graceful three-fold windows. This palace was built in 1216. In 1339 it was repaired and enlarged by Agostino di Giovanni, Agostino del Rosso and Cecco di Casino, and again in

Fig. 7 - Fonte Gaia (the Gay Fountain).

modern times. In the Middle Ages the rhomboidal tower which rises from the centre of the building was so high that it rivalled with the « Mangia » tower. It contains the Chapel of Blessed Ambrogio Sansedoni, built in 1692, where the Saint had his bedroom. On the altar is a bas-relief of the Saint and his vision of Virgin Mary, produced by Giuseppe Mazzuoli. On the walls are some good bronze bas-reliefs by Massimiliano Soldani. The vault is the work of Antonio Domenico Gabbiani.

Now, let us go back to the centre of the square to have a better view of the Town Hall.

THE TOWN HALL
(Palazzo Pubblico)

This building is a true masterpiece of Tuscan Gothic architecture. Just as grandiose as Palazzo della Signoria in Florence, it is even richer, more graceful and elegant owing to the curved facade to the effect of the two different coloured materials used, the ogival three-fold windows instead of double ones and to the greater slenderness of the whole. It was built in the lapse of time from 1288 to 1309 probably to Agostino di Giovanni and Agnolo di Ventura's designs. In 1327 the right side was enlarged and the prisons were built; in 1340-42 a large hall called sala del Consiglio della Campana was added (the Hall of the Bell Council). The large disk with the name of Christ used as the emblem of St. Bernardine which is still now high up on the central part of the facade was painted by Battista di Niccolò da Padova in 1425 and decorated with rays, letters and friezes by Turino di Sano and his son Giovanni. In 1560 the coat-of-arms of the Medici was added and in the 16th. century the top floor was built over the lateral wings. The whole building was restored during the past century (fig. 8).

THE EXTERIOR

The facade is slightly curved. The central portion is three storeys high but the lateral wings only two.

The lower part up to the first floor is made of stone whilst the upper part is brick; the whole facade is battlemented. The door and all the windows on the ground floor are surmonted with Sienese arches (that is, a pointed arch over a flat rounded arch); the first and second floors have threefold Gothic windows, the third floor, instead, has double windows. All of them are surmounted with an ogival spandrel decorated with the « Balzana » (the black and white coat-of-arms of the town). On the left hand side of the facade stands the CAPPELLA DI PIAZZA (fig. 9) which was built as a thanksgiving after the great plague in the year 1348. It has the shape of a loggia with three arches, started in 1352 by Domenico di Agostino and completed in 1376 by Giovanni di Cecco; from 1468 to 1470 Antonio Federighi modified the arches and the little roof. All the statues on the pillars date back to the years from 1377 to 1381. From the pillar on the right hand side going towards the opposite side they are: in the upper niche, the statue of *San Giacomo Maggiore* by Bartolomeo di Tommè and Mariano di Angelo; *San Giovanni Battista* (above) and *San Giacomo Minore* (below), *San Pietro* (above) by the same artists, *San Bartolomeo* (below) by Lando di Stefano and *San Tommaso* by Giovanni di Turino.

The bas-reliefs on the front are imitations by Enea Becheroni (1848) of the original Pisan-style work of the duecento no longer existent. The iron wrought gate is the work of Conte di Lelio Orlandi and Petruccio di Betto (15th. century). The fresco over the altar representing the *Madonna with the Eternal Father and Saints is* by Sodoma (1537), restored in 1951.

Behind the Cappella di Piazza rises the slender and graceful TORRE DEL MANGIA (Mangia tower). It is 102 metres high to the top of the lightning conductor and is called after a certain Giovanni di Duccio, nicknamed *Mangiaguadagni* or simply *Mangia*, the first watchman whose business was to strike the hours. Very soon a wooden automaton was set up for that purpose, later on replaced with a metal one and finally with a travertine figure that continued the job till 1780. The tower was built by Minuccio and Francesco di Rinaldo from

Fig. 8 - The Town Hall.

Perugia in the years from 1338 to 1348. It is all made of brick except the top part with the graceful bell chamber and elegant battlements which are made of stone. The model of the stone work was made by Lippo Memmi in 1341 and built by Agostino di Giovanni. Right on the top within an iron housing is the big bell which was cast by Girolamo Santoni from Fano and Giovanni Battista Salvini from Siena; it weighs 6.764 kg. and was placed there in 1666. It is generally called *Campanone* which means the big bell but, as it was baptised with the name of Maria Assunta, the Sienese often call it *Sunto*. From the very first its solemn tones were heard only on great occasions, happy or sad, in civic or national life. The first clock placed inside the tower was made by a certain maestro Perino in 1360 but is was completely re-made in 1425 by a Jesuit called Giovanni da Milano.

Fig. 9 - The Town Hall Chapel in the « Campo »

Fig. 10 - The Courtyard of the Podestà and the « Mangia » tower.

On the right hand side of the Cappella di Piazza is the charming CORTILE DEL PODESTÀ (The court-yard of the Podestà) built in the year 1325, restored in 1929. From here there is a very good view of the tower (fig. 10). The coat-of-arms of the ancient « Reggitori » (regents of the town) are let into the walls all around the court-yard and there is also the remains of a beautiful fourteenth-century fresco of the *Madonna with two angels;* parts of the stone statue of the *Mangia* are still to be seen (fig. 14). At the bottom of the court is the entrance to the THEATRE OF THE RINNUOVATI (once the *Great Council Hall of the Republic*) built in 1560 by Riccio, completely rebuilt by Bibbiena in 1753 and modernized in 1951). A small door is in the wall just beneath the fresco on the left hand side; it leads to the top of the MANGIA TOWER from where may be enjoyed a most delightful view of the Sienese country-side right down to the hill called Montagnola and as far as Mount Amiata.

Coming out of the Cortile del Podestà turn to the left and pass through the doorway the arch of which is decorated with a delightful ornamental frieze of foliage surmounted with a statue and a basrelief in a lunette representing two *she-wolves* and a crowned *rampant lion*. It leads into the entrance hall. Near the portal stands a column bearing a gilt-lead copy of the Sienese *She-wolf* produced by Giovanni e Lorenzo di Turino in 1429. The original has now been transferred to the Civic Museum.

THE INTERIOR

On the walls of the entrance hall (where the admission tickets to the monumental rooms are sold) are two delightful bronze brackets, formerly in the Palazzo del Magnifico, which are the work of Giacomo Cozzarelli.

THE GROUND FLOOR, actually used as offices, can be visited only by special permit. Entering the first hall, on the left wall is a fresco of the *Sienese in the Holy Land* by Rutilio Manetti. From here pass into the second hall which leads into the rooms themselves. Near the wall are two 14th century stone *She-wolves* ascribed to Giovanni Pisano, and *Moses* by Federighi in the 15th. century; on the right wall beneath the third vault see the fresco of

Pietro Alessandrino with Blessed Ambrogio Sansedoni and Blessed Andrea Gallerani, by Sano di Pietro in 1446.

In the second room, on the right, is a fresco representing the *Madonna with the Holy Babe and Saints* by Sodoma in 1537, and on the vault some good seventeenth-century frescoes. In the third room on the left wall is Sano di Pietro's splendid fresco representing the *Coronation of Virgin Mary, Angels, St. Bernardine and St. Catherine* (1445). The vault was painted in the 17th. century but the delightful carved bench is a 15th. century work. In the fourth room we see Sodoma's *Ressurection* and Arcangelo Salimbeni's *banner*. In the first room on the left side is the « Cappella dei Nove », (the chapel of the Nine Authorities). On the vault we see *Christ in glory with five Cherubs*, by Simone Martini and his pupils in 1339; the portraits of *Four Evangelists* ascribed to Antonio Veneziano in 1370; the portraits of *Sant'Antonio d'Aquino, Santo Antonio Abate* and *Blessed Andrea Gallerani*, probably painted in the same year, and last a fragment of the *Annunciation*. Near the third room is a column bearing an *Imperial Eagle and two Cherubs*, and a fresco by Sodoma; inside this room is a good but rather spoilt fresco by Vecchietta representing the *Madonna della Misericordia*.

Now the visitor will be once more in the entrance hall where is the staircase to the upper rooms.

THE FIRST FLOOR. On the right hand side of the entrance is the SALA DEL MAPPAMONDO (the Hall of the Map) so called because Ambrogio Lorenzetti painted a Map on the walls, which no longer exists. This room contains the two most beautiful frescoes in Siena, both by Simone Martini : *La Maestà* and *Guido Riccio da Fogliano*. Unfortunately they are spoilt like those in the next room called Lorenzetti's Hall. This is partly due to the colours and the technique but mostly to the dampness of the walls and to the action of time. However, what is still visible of these two most splendid paintings is more than enough to excite interest and enthusiasm and to help us conceive their original beauty. All these frescoes have been restored.

At the bottom of the room, on the left within a decorative frame is Simone Martini's *Maestà* (Majesty), It is one of his early works and bears his signature and the date (1315), nevertheless it is astonishingly perfect. The « Madonna » is seated upon a throne under a canopy (fig. 11) with the Holy Child in her arms and two Angels are offering her flowers. At her sides are the patron Saints of Siena Sant'Ansano, San Vittorio, San Savino and San Crescenzio surround-

Fig. 11 - The Town Hall - Simone Martini: *Maestà*
(Majesty - a detail).

ed by Apostles and Saints (in all, thirty two figures),
eight of which are bearing the canopy. Although this fresco obviously derives from a similar composition by Duccio,
now in the Museum of the Cathedral (see page 89), the

Fig. 12 - The Town Hall - Simone Martini: *Guido Riccio da Fogliano*
(a detail).

stylistic interpretation of the subject is most personal. Here
we see a Gothic chair richly decorated with little triple-
windows and lobes instead of Duccio's massive Romanesque
throne, the figures are grouped together in one harmonious
whole whilst Duccio placed the Madonna with the Saints
and Angels in the centre and the Apostles above them, almost like statues in little tabernacles; here, instead of the
unreal glitter of the gold background we see a pretty blue
that reminds us of the sky. Even if the features of some of
the personages, their heads and their expression (here,
much sweeter and not so solemn) are still connected with
the art of Duccio di Buoninsegna, they have a kind of fluidity formerly unknown; this marks the appearance of something new which was to reveal itself as Simone Martini's
artistic signature. Most interesting is, for instance, the waving outline of the multicoloured canopy, the movement of
some of the heads, the attitude of the kneeling Saints and,
above all, the two exquisite Angels carrying baskets of
flowers in their delicately modelled hands, as graceful as
arabesques.

Fig. 13 - The Town Hall - Ambrogio Lorenzetti: *The Good
Government* (a detail).

High up on the opposite wall is another of Simone Martini's masterpieces : *Guido Riccio da Fogliano on his way to the siege of Montemassi* (1328). Here the artistic inspiration is quite different but just as striking. This fresco was painted in 1329. The Sienese captain portrayed sideways on his steed with a Commander's baton in his hand is placed in the centre of the picture (fig. 12). The landscape is bare and the colours dull (two hills and some turreted walls in the distance with a few waving banners) but the disposition of the elements is so happy, the central figure so real that the scene can hardly be forgotten. The power of Martini's style is so strong that we almost seem to hear the noise of the horse's hoofs on the hard ground in the silent country side. The colours of the horseman's coat-of-mail and of the cover and saddle of the horse are rich and brilliant : rich tones of blond and orange with black chequer decorations, a grand contrast to the rest of the picture which shows but the dark blue colour of the sky and the greys of the ground.

Above the arches are two frescoes : On the right, *The Sienese troops against the Florentines at the battle of Poggio Imperiale, near Poggibonsi*, by Giovanni di Cristoforo and Francesco di Andrea (1480) ; on the left, *The Battle of the Sienese against the English Company of the « Cappello » at Sinalunga*, by Lippo Vanni (1370).

On the pillars there are some other good frescoes, from right to left, as follows : The portraits of *two Sienese Saints* (Beato Andrea Gallerani and Beato Ambrogio Sansedoni) belonging to the school of Riccio (16th. century) ; next an inspired picture of *St. Catherine* by Vecchietta (1461) ; then comes *St. Bernardine*, by Sano di Pietro (1460) and last *Beato Bernardo Tolomei*, by Sodoma (1533).

Beneath the fresco representing Guido Riccio da Fogliano there is another *Maestà* (Madonna and Child) painted on a wooden panel ; the lobes are decorated with Angels and *Christ between two Angels* is painted in the finial. It is known as the « Madonna di Guido » because it was painted by Guido da Siena. The attitude and the features of the figures and the gold ground show a strong Byzantine influence though some Romanesque elements are evident. This is the most important picture to which all the studies on the very earliest Sienese painting refer (see also the *Madonna dagli occhi grossi* - the large-eyed Madonna - now in the Museum of the Cathedral; page 90). This panel is signed and dated 1221. Towards the end of the 13th. century a pupil of Duccio's repainted the head and the hands both of the Madonna and of the Holy Child, but in 1950 they were restored to their original state.

AMBROGIO LORENZETTI (Siena, ...1318-1348)

Gli effetti del Buon Governo in città (particolare) (Palazzo Pubblico)

Effets du Bon Gouvernement dans la ville (détail) (Palais Public)

The Effects of Good Government on the Town (detail) (Town Hall).

Die Erfolge der guten Regierung in der Stadt (Ausschnitt) (Rathaus)

I.

Two figures by Sodoma are frescoed on the right and on the left hand side : *Sant'Ansano in the act of baptizing, and San Vittorio.*

Now pass into the SALA DELLA PACE O DEI NOVE (the Hall of Peace, or of the Nine) so called because it was once the seat of the government of the «Noveschi» (the Nine Rulers) to whom Ambrogio Lorenzetti dedicated the greatest cycle of profane frescoes of the Middle Ages (1337-1339).

On the wall opposite the windows is : *Il Buon Governo* (the Good Government) symbolized by a noble *King* dressed in the colours of the Balzana, seated amidst the *six Virtues* (the last on the left resting on the corner of the divan is *Peace;* her features are noble and classic, her expression sweet and thoughtful (fig. 13). The *three Theological Virtues* are hovering over the *King;* at his feet are two cherubs and the She-wolf of Siena, though nothing can be seen of it but the muzzle. Lower down is represented the Sienese army with a group of prisoners in chains. In the left corner of this fresco we see *Justice* seated upon a throne holding her scales attended by *two genii (Commutative Justice* and *Distributive Justice)* ; her eyes are turned towards *Wisdom* from whom she draws inspiration. Two ribbons coming from the scales are gathered by *Concord* (a figure of remarkable majesty) whose business is to keep human desires balanced by means of her plane, and then are handed to the 24 *Counselors* (among whom concord reigns) on their way to the *King (the Good Government).*

At the bottom of the painting, placed within panels are the figures of *Grammar* and *Dialectic.* Between them is the verse explanation of the scene, very likely by the painter himself. *Questa santa Virtù la dove regge - Induce a unità gli animi molti : - E questi a ciò rivolti - Un ben comun per lor Signor si fanno : - Lo qual per governar suo stato, elegge - Di non tener giamma' gli occhi rivolti - Da lo splendor de' volti - Dele Virtù che torno allui stanno : - Per questo con triunfo allui si danno - Censi, tributi e signorie di terre : - Per questo, sanza guerre, - Seguita poi ogni civil effetto, - utile, necessario e di diletto.* This inscription says : This holy virtù unites the souls whose aim is unity. To rule well the King never turns his eyes away from the Virtues seated around him. This is the reason why taxes, fees and lands are paid to him without any fighting. Lower down is a scroll bearing the signature : AMBROSIUS LAURENTII DE SENIS HIC PINXIT UTRINQUE.

On the right wall we see *Gli effetti del buon governo in città* (the effects of Good Government on the town) : Siena is represented with her winding streets, her squares, her turreted palaces enlivened with processions of horsemen escorting rich nuptials, dancing maidens and busy marts (see the coloured plate on the cover). Then *Gli effetti del buon governo in campagna* (the effects of Good Government on the country) : peasants are busy ploughing and harvesting the rich crops and fishermen and huntsmen are mingled with them. Between the two scenes is the figure of *Safety* bearing a scroll with a few verses summarising the theme of the composition.

Senza paura ognuom franco camini - E lavorando semini ciascuno, - Mentre che tal Comuno - Manterrà questa donna in signoria, - Ch'el ha levata a' rei ogni balía. (Do not fear, and work and sow peacefully whilst this maiden is mistress because she has deprived the wicked of their power).

Along the wall runs another inscription : *Volgiete gli occhi a rimirar costei, - Voi che reggete, ch'è qui figurata, - E per sue ciellenza coronata : - La qual sempre a ciascun suo diritto rende. - Guardate quanti ben vengan da lei - E come è dolce vita e riposata - Quella de la città du' servata - Questa che più d'altra risplende. - Ella guarda e difende - Chi lei onora, e lor nutrica et pascie : - Et agl'iniqui dar debite bene.* (Admire her wearing her crown. She is fair to every one, Look how many run to her, and how easy and sweet life is in the town she rules. She watches over those who honour her, and punishes the guilty).

On the left wall : the ruined fresco representing the *Cattivo Governo* (the Bad Government) sorrounded with the figures of *Tyranny, Fraud, Cruelty, Deceit, Anger, Discord* and *Perfidy; Justice* is in chains with a very hurt expression. Above her are *Avarice, Pride* and *Vainglory.* On the left, almost detached is the fresco representing the *Effetti del cattivo Governo* (the effects of Bad Government), also in two separate scenes : *Malgoverno nella città e in campagna* (Bad Government inside the town and Bad Government in the Country). Plundering and scenes of violence are represented everywhere on a desolate background. The verse caption is presented by the figure of *Fear* who says : *Per volere el ben proprio in questa terra - Sommess'è la Giustizia a Tirannia : - Unde per questa vita - Non passa alcun senza dubbio di morte - Ché fuor si robba e dentro da le porte.* (Through our greed in this world of ours Giustice is overcome by Tyrany. No one is without fear because robberies go on everywhere). At the bottom on the frame is this other inscription : *...e per effetto - Che dove è Tirannia è gran sospetto, - Guerre, rapine, tradimenti e inganni - Prendansi signoria sopra di lei - E pongasi la mente e lo intelletto - In tener sempre a Iustizia soggetto - Ciascun per ischivar sì scuri danni, - Abbattendo i' tiranni : - E chi turbar la vuol, sia per suo merto, - Discacciat'*

e diserto, - Insieme con qualunque s'ha seguacie, - Fortifi-
cando lei per nostra pace. (Wherever tyrany exists there is
fear, wars, treason and deceit. To avoid unhappiness every-
body must bow to Justice. Banished be all those who are
against her, for peace's sake).

In the frieze the figure of *Nero* in the act of killing himself can still be seen and also the scene of the *Agression
of Caracalla and Geta.* The coats-of-arms of the Commune
and of the people run along the borders together with
the symbols of Arts and Trades; another inscription
is at the bottom of the fresco: *Là dove sta legata la Ju-
stitia - Nessun al ben comun già may s'acorda, - Ne tira
a dritta corda - Però convien che Tirannia sormonti: - La
qual per adempir la sua nequizia, - Nullo voler né operar
aiscorda - Da la natura lorda - De' vitii che con lei son qui
congionti. - Questa caccia color che al ben son pronti, -
E cniama a se ciascun che a male intende. - Questa sempre
difende - Chi sforza, o robba o chi odiasse pace: - Unde
ogni terra sua inculta giace.* (Where Justice is kept a prisoner no good can ever be. Tyrany is mistress. She favours
the wicked and persues the good).

The importance of this cycle of frescoes is due to
their excellent style rather than to symbolism, at that
time suggested by scholastic philosophy. Here Ambrogio
Lorenzetti brought to evidence the plastic and figurative
values (not the linear musical values of Simone Martini in
the preceding hall), the architectonic values (see the fine
synthesis of mediaeval Siena) and the pictorical values of
the landscape. Most delightful are some of the details of
the figures of the women, here so full of beauty and clasical
dignity with something strange and mysterious about them
(for istance, the figure of *Peace* and that of *Concord* in the
scene of the Good Government); some of the groups such
as the maidens dancing at the sound of their cymbals and
the cavalcade escorting the bride in the *Effects of Good
Government,* are amazingly bright. As to the colours, as
far as can be gathered from the now corroded frescoes,
blacks and reds prevailed and, generally speaking, Lorenzetti seems to have preferred contrasting colours to delicate
blending tones.

From the Sala della Pace (the Hall of Peace) walk into
the SALA DEI PILASTRI (the Hall of the Pillars) where there
is a diptych by Neroccio di Bartolommeo Landi dedicated
to St. Bernardine (on one side: *St. Bernardine preaching in
Piazza del Campo;* on the other: *St. Bernardine recovering
a possessed woman*) and a fine 14th. century triptych with
figures of *Saints,* belonging to the Sienese school. Remarkable is a huge coffer in which the money of the « Biccher-

na » (the administrative offices of the Commune) was kept, and also a few other Renaissance coffers, the bell of the Church of S. Cristoforo which was rung at the battle of Monteaperti (1260), bronze Crucifixes, a wax *Crucifixion* belonging to the 17th. century and a Gold Rose which was given to Siena by Pope Pius II in the year 1459.

Now, return to the Hall of the Map and enter the ANTI-CAPPELLA and the CAPPELLA (the Ante-Chapel and the Chapel) which are on the right hand side. They are both entirely decorated with frescoes by Taddeo di Bartolo (1407-1414). On the left wall of the antechapel there is a huge *St. Christopher* and all around are the figures of some famous personages taken from Roman history, of pagan divinities, philosophers and Virtues. Inside the CHA-PEL the Master painted scenes taken from the life of Virgin Mary including her *Death* and *Assumption*. Though these paintings do not reach a very high aesthetic level they are remarkable for their many happy chromatic combinations. The entrance to this Chapel has a very fine wrought iron gate which is the work of Niccolò di Paolo and Giovanni di Vito (1437). The delightful quire is placed along two of the walls. It is composed of 22 carved Gothic stalls decorated with scenes representing the Articles of the *Creed,* attributed to Domenico di Niccolò who was afterwards called « de' Cori » in honour of his work (1415-1428). The sculptured altar is due to Marrina; it is adorned with a very good composition by Sodoma: *The Holy Family and St. Leonard.* This work dates back to 1536 and is a very good sample of bright colouring, correct chiaroscuro and pleasant landscape. The wooden lamp is Gothic and was produced by Cecco di Ciucca in 1370 with the help of the painter Cristoforo da Cosona. The richly carved organ is the work of Giovanni Piffero and Ghino di Antonio (1524). The Holy water basin on the right decorated with the figures of the *Saviour and Angels* is by Giovanni di Turino (1434).

Returning to the Chapel, on the right hand side is the SALA DEI CARDINALI (the Hall of the Cardinals). The walls are decorated with frescoes representing *Saints* (14th.-15th. centuries) (The fresco over the door of the Sala di Balia is ascribed to Ambrogio Lorenzetti) ; of the wooden Crucifixes the painted one belongs to the 14th. century, the other to the 15th.; the panel representing *Virgin Mary and the Holy Child* is believed to be the work of Matteo di Giovanni though ascribed to Guidoccio Cozzarelli. Near the thrid door are two wooden statues of *Saints* by some artist of Antonio Federighi's time.

On the left hand side, after the Hall of the Cardinals

is the SALA DEL CONCISTORO (the Concistory Hall). The very elegant marble portal is the work of Bernardo Gamberelli, nicknamed Rossellino (1468) and the carved wooden jambs of Domenico di Niccolò de' Cori. The beautiful frescoes on the vault represent *heroic scenes taken from Roman and Greek history,* so Valerio Massimo tells us, and are the work of Domenico Beccafumi nicknamed Mecarino, from 1529 to 1535. Here the master indulges in pale, radiant misty colours, with rich chiaroscuro and tones : the perspective is often audacious. In the middle of the vault stands *Justice* with *Concord* and *Patriotism* beside her. Over the portal is a picture by Luca Giordano: *Solomon's judgment,* of great interest for the beauty of the colours. The three large 18th. century tapestries on the walls are most remarkable; they come from Gobelins and represent : *the Allegory of Earth, Air and Fire.* (The fourth of the series is the *Allegory of Water* now to be seen in the Museum of Tapestries of Florence). The five smaller ones, also representing allegories, were made in Florence.

Right in front of the portal of the Concistory Hall is the SALA DI BALIA (the Hall of Power). It is divided into two parts by an arch and is frescoed all around. On the vault are *sixteen Virtues* by Martino di Bartolommeo (1408). On the walls are scenes from the life of Pope Alexander III (1159-1181) who descended from the Bandinelli family of Siena. They are the work of Spinello Aretino (1407). These compositions have no great artistic value but they are pleasing because of the way the stories are presented and for the striking intensity of the enamel-like colours.

On the first half of the wall opposite the windows we see : high up, *Alexander receiving the Pontifical Crown*; below : *Alexander commits the Sword to the Doge of Venice* (this one is considered as the best fresco of all for the accurate details). On the other half of the wall we see : high up, *the Foundation of Alexandria; below, Barbarossa Submits to Alexander.* In the lunettes facing the door are : on the right hand side *Alexander forgiving Prince Otto; on* the left, *The Canonization of Canute the Dane.* All along the wall is the scene of *Alexander on his way back to Rome with Barbarossa and the Doge of Venice* (most interesting are the face of the Pope, the landscape and the architectural background). On the right side of the wall where the windows are we see : *a German Messenger handing a message to the King of France who is seated near the Pope;* on the left : *the Doge presents Prince Otto as a prisoner to Alexander.* On the entrance wall, in the lunettes on the left hand side : *Interview with Ludovico VII, King of France;* on the right : *disguised as a*

Carthusian Alexander quits Rome; below, *the Venetian Fleet beats the Fleet of Barbarossa at Punta Savore.* In the lunettes over the arch on the left hand side of the entrance door : *Anti-Pope Victor IV is Crowned at the presence of Barbarossa;* on the right : *Alexander receiving homages at Ninfa.* Towards the exit door on the left : *the Lateran Synod;* on the right *the pyre of the four Anti-Popes.* The carved door on the right is the work of Domenico di Niccolò de' Cori, and the wooden throne, of Barna di Turino (1410).

In front of the exit door, across the landing is the SALA MONUMENTALE (the Monumental Hall) sometimes called *the Hall of Vittorio Emanuele II.* It was frescoed during the last century by the best Sienese painter of that time (1886-1891) with scenes representing the most important moments of Vittorio Emanuele's life, when the unity of Italy was achieved.

In the middle of the vault Alessandro Franchi painted *Italy Triumphant;* on the fourteen smaller vaults are the figures of the precursors of Italian Unity. On the walls, starting from the left corner, right wall : *Vittorio Emanuele II meets Radetzky after the battle of Novara* (by Pietro Aldi) ; *the battle of Palestro* (Amos Cassioli) ; *the battle of San Martino* (Amos Cassioli) ; *the King and Garibaldi on the bridge of Teano* (P. Aldi) ; *the King receives from the hands of Michele Caetani, Duca di Sermoneta, the document containing the Plebiscite of Rome.* This scene is represented inside Palazzo Pitti and was painted by Cesare Maccari ; *the King's Funeral in the Pantheon* (Cesare Maccari). The statue at the bottom of the room represents *Sorrow* and was produced by Emilio Gallori. All around are the marble busts of politicians and artists of the 19th. century, respectively the work of Tito Sarrocchi, Enea Becheroni, Giovanni Magi and Arnoldo Prunai. In the walnut cabinet is the uniform worn by Vittorio Emanuele II at the Battle of San Martino on June 24, 1859.

Now go up the first flight of steps leading to the upper rooms. On the landing is the entrance to the MUSEO CIVICO where the moulds of Iacopo della Quercia's best works are ranged (see the moulds made for the portal of the Church of San Petronio in Bologna and for the famous sepulchre of Ilaria del Carretto in Lucca). On the top of the stairs there is a LOGGIA from where a most beautiful panorama of the Sienese countryside may be enjoyed. Here are the remnants of Jacopo della Quercia's *Fonte Gaia* (Gay Fountain). Though ruined and corroded by time these remnants still show the master's skill and powerful style, and the grace and dignity he was able to put into his figures. The two lovely statues at the sides of the fountain are *Justice* and *Charity*, the latter carried out with the collaboration of Francesco di Vaidambrino. The statues are ranged in the same order as in the fountain now in the Campo square (see p. 38). In front of the entrance is a fine expressive fresco by Ambrogio Lorenzetti : *Virgin Mary and the Holy Child* (1340). From the Loggia go to the SALA DELLE ADUNANZE (Assembly Hall) where there are two good pictures by Amos Cassioli : the *Oath of Pontida* and *Provenzano Salvani in the Campo Square* (1875). On the left are other four rooms with some interesting pictures by Alessandro Casolani, Ventura Salimbeni and Bernardo Strozzi. In the adjoining *Museum* there are prints pictures and plans relating to the history of Siena and of the Contrade. In room 1 : Sienese iconography ; room 2 : prints of the Palio and other games ; room 3 : history and topography of the town ; room 4 : models of the old fountains and of Salicotto. To go up to the tower call the door keeper.

Fig. 14 - The Courtyard of the « Podestà ». *The statue of the « Mangia » and a ruined 14th century fresco.*

Itinerary II

FROM PIAZZA DEL CAMPO TO THE CATHEDRAL SQUARE AND TO THE BAPTISTERY

[Loggia della Mercanzia (The market Loggia) - Palazzo Chigi Saracini - Duomo (The Cathedral) - Museo dell'Opera Metropolitana (The Museum of the Cathedral) - Chiesa e Spedale di Santa Maria della Scala (The Church and Hospital of Santa Maria della Scala) - Battistero (The Baptistery)].

From piazza del Campo the « *Vicolo di S. Pietro* » (St. Peter's Lane) leads to the « *Croce del Travaglio* » which is the junction of three streets: Banchi di Sopra, Banchi di Sotto and Via di Città; at the time of the Republic this was the spot where barricades were set up against the cavalry of the invaders. At the beginning of Via di Città, on the left is the LOGGIA DELLA MERCANZIA (the market Loggia), once the seat of the Tribunal of traders. It has three arches on one side but only one on each of the shorter sides and was built in the years from 1417 to 1429 by Sano di Matteo. Its style is that of the Renaissance but the ornamental niches with the statues of Saints are still Gothic (fig. 16). In the 17th. century a new storey was built over the arches. The pillars looking on to Via di Città bear four statues: the two lateral ones represent *St. Paul* (on the right) and *St. Peter* (on the left) and are the work of Vecchietta; the two central ones represent *San Vittore* and *Sant'Ansano* and are the work of Federighi. The vaults - restored in 1953 - are ornamented with stucco and frescoes. The first vault was painted by Pastorino dei Pastorini (1549-1551), the second and third by Lorenzo Rustici nicknamed « Rustico », and his pupils (1563-1564). On the right, under the Loggia is a very good marble bench decorated with *the figures of illustrious*

Roman personages by Federighi (1464): another marble bench is on the left, ornamented with the sculptured fi-of Urbano da Cortona. The wrought iron gate was drawn gures of the four *Cardinal Virtues,* due to the master hand by Augusto Corbi in 1887. The facade looking on to the « Campo » was drawn by Domenico di Niccolò dei Cori in 1417 and restored as we see it now by Fuga in 1763. Walking along Via di Città where are many imposing me-diaeval buildings the first corner on the left is that of the « Costarella dei Barbieri »; on the corner is the stone tower of the Rustici family, called the TOWER OF the « SETTE SEGHINELLE »; it has four orders of blind double windows, each surmounted with a pointed arch. The street then becomes narrower and a severe but picturesque background of palaces comes into sight: no. 75 is PALAZZO PATRIZI, now the seat of the « Intro-nati » Academy; no. 89 the splendid PALAZZO CHI-GI SARACINI, once Marescotti (fig. 15) with its curved

Fig. 15 - Palazzo Chigi Saracini.   Fig. 16 - Loggia della Mercanzia.

facade. It dates back to the 13th. century but in 1787 it was enlarged and in 1914- 1922 restored by Arturo Viligiardi.

The austerity of the architecture is mitigated by the bright tone of the stone. The light from the narrow strip of sky enlivens the weather beaten walls in a surprising way. The slender triple Gothic windows contribute much to the grandeur and decorative beauty typical to the Sienese architecture. The left side of the palace, the facade up to the first floor, and the tower (from the top of which Cerreto Ceccolini announced the victory of the Sienese militia at the battle of Monteaperti) are made of stone, all the rest is brick. The triple windows are surmounted with the coats-of-arms of noble families, bull's eyes and pointed arches.

This palace is now the seat of the CHIGIANA MUSIC ACADEMY which is an Istitution for high classes of music founded by Count Guido Chigi Saracini in 1930; regular clasess of international renown are held every year from July 15th. to September 15th. From November 22nd. to the end of May concerts are offered for charity purposes; this special activity dates back to 1922 and is known by the name of MICAT IN VERTICE. The Chigiana Music Academy started the SIENESE MUSICAL WEEK which runs every year in July.

Inside the entrance to Palazzo Chigi is the statue of Pope Giulius II della Rovere the son of Cristofora Saracini, by Fulvio Signorini in 1609, and on the walls are many commemorative inscriptions, coats-of-arms and a bas-relief dedicated to Sapìa dei Salvani (the wife of Ghinibaldo Saracini) the famous Sienese gentlewoman mentioned by Dante in the XII Canto of *Purgatory*. Down one side of the courtyard runs a portico; in the middle is a well-head. The vaults of the portico were painted with grotesque figures by Giorgio di Giovanni.

THE INTERIOR (for admission apply to the door keeper). Elegance and good taste are remarkable everywhere; some rooms were decorated by Arturo Viligiardi in 1922. The concert hall, bright and luminous is in a sober 18th. century style; on the vault is a fresco by A. Viligiardi representing *the Return of the Sienese after the battle of Monteaperti*. The music library is decorated with a fresco

by Emilio Ambron representing the *Encounter of Sapia
and Dante in Purgatory* (1954). Most interesting is the collection of old instruments. Among the pictures are ancient Byzantine Madonne as well as masterpieces by the
best modern painters : Maccari, Belloni, Cassioli, Viligiardi.
The art of the trecento, of the Renaissance and of the 17th.
century is also well represented ; the most important works
are : a marble basrelief by Donatello representing *the Madonna and Holy Child;* a painted wooden statue by Jacopo
della Quercia representing the *Deposition from the Cross;* a
sketch by the same artist for Fonte Gaia (the Gay Fountain) ; a *painted Crucifix* belonging to Berlighieri's school ;
a diptych belonging to the school of Giotto ; *St. Paul* by
Simone Martini ; *the Magi; the Madonna with St. John;
St. Martin; the Madonna with four Saints,* all by Sassetta :
the Madonna and Holy Child, by Matteo di Giovanni ; *the Madonna and Holy Child,* by Neroccio di Bar-
to'omeo Landi ; a most beautiful *Madonna and Holy
Child between two Angels,* by Botticelli ; *the Madonna adoring the Holy Child,* by Lorenzo di Credi ; *Infant Jesus,* by
Perugino ; *the Madonna and Holy Child,* by Pinturicchio ; *the Madonna and Holy Child,* by Pontormo ; *a
Knight,* by Sebastiano del Piombo ; *the Holy Family,* by
Cima da Conegliano ; *the figures of two monks,* by Dürer ;
other paintings by Sodoma, Beccafumi, school of Leonardo, Rustichino, Pacchiarotti, Brescianino, Peruzzi, Salvator
Rosa, and other artists of the Renaissance and later periods.

Opposite Palazzo Chigi Saracini is PALAZZO PICCOLO-
MINI, otherwise called « DELLE PAPESSE » because it was
built by Catherine, Pope Pius. II's sister. It dates back
to 1460-1465 and was designed by Bernardo Rossellino
with rustic bosses up to the first storey and double windows in the upper part. Actually it is the seat of the
Bank of Italy. On the corner of Via del Castoro is PA-
LAZZO MARSILI (no. 130) a brick building with three rows
of triple windows, built in 1444 over a pre-existing house
by Luca di Bartolo da Bagnacavallo and restored in 1876
by Giuseppe Partini. A few steps further on is Piazza Postierla; on the right corner is the CASA-TORRE FORTEGUER-
RI (the tower-house of the Forteguerri family). Opposite
is a marble column with a Sienese She-wolf and a very
graceful wrought iron flagstaff of the 15th century. On
the right hand side is PALAZZO CHIGI (later half of the
16th. century). Turning to the right is Via del Capitano

with the PALAZZO DEL CAPITANO DI GIUSTIZIA. This palace was built in the 13th. century and restored according to the traditions of the Italian Renaissance by Luca di Bartolo da Bagnacavallo in 1449. In 1854 Giulio Rossi restored it to its original state. More than half of it is made of stone but the battlemented top part is brick. The lower part has nine Sienese arches each one surmounted with a double window; a row of little arches on triangular ledges crowns the whole, decorated with the coat-of-arms and names of the Magistrates and Commanders-in-chief who dwelt there or had their headquarters inside the building. Of particular interest is the *courtyard* and staircase with the *Lion of the People*. Just after this imposing building is

THE CATHEDRAL SQUARE
(Piazza del Duomo)

This square is limited on the left by the facade of the Church and Hospital of Santa Maria della Scala, on the right by the Palazzo del Governo and by the walls of the new Cathedral, and in front by the palace of the Archbishop; in the middle is

THE CATHEDRAL
(Duomo)

This splendid building is like a luminous poetical hymn in praise of God expressed in marble. It is one of the most beautiful Italian cathedrals built in the Romanesque-Gothic style (fig. 17). The lower part of the facade and the interior is Romanesque with some evidence of the Gothic influence but the upper part of the facade, the way the pillars are inserted at the corners and the general appearance of the whole prospect is pure Gothic. Many other architectural elements are Gothic, as well, for instance, the vaults oer the nave and the double windows on the sides. The superimposition of the two styles is due to the fact that the long time the Cathedral took to build (from the 13th. century to

Fig. 17 – An aerial view of the Cathedral. On the right are the arches and the of the New Cathedral.

the 14th.) corresponds in history of art to the period of transition from the Romanesque style to the Gothic. This same reason and the many alterations that took place in the plans account for certain structural irregularities which, however, do not spoil the harmony of the whole.

First it is better to consider the whole building from different places so as to have a general idea of its aspect. From the right hand corner of the square it is possible to see the whole facade, the right side, the belfry and a part of the right nave of the new Cathedral which was left unfinished.

The vicissitudes in connection with the origin and the completion of the Cathedral are many. As far back as the 11th. century a smaller abbey stood exactly on the same spot. The temple as it is now to be seen was started by anonymous artists who, most probably, drew inspiration from the buildings belonging to the Monks of Cluny, above all from the Abbey of Sant'Antimo in the late half of the 12th. century. By the first years of the 13th. century the nave the aisles and the front and side walls (the lower part) were already finished off. By the end of the same century the dome, the apse and the peribolo were also finished (though later on they suffered damage and were rebuilt).

From 1258 to 1285 the Cistertian Monks took over the administration of the work but did not interfere with the architecture. They called Nicola Pisano to Siena and ordered him the marble pulpit which is one of his best masterpieces. Nicola's son Giovanni, with the help of some minor artists, carried out the marble work on the lower part of the facade. Siena was just then at the climax of her prosperity and the cathedral as it was seemed inadequate; plans were then started to lengthen the apse towards Valle Piatta after having demolished the existing apse. Camaino di Crescentino was called for the purpose but very soon even this solution seemed unsatisfactory and the building of a new Cathedral was considered, a grandiose building to compete with Santa Maria del Fiore in Florence.

The actual Cathedral should have become the transept of the new one. Many plans were made but only Lan-

Fig. 18 - The Cathedral - The facade.

do di Pietro's were chosen and he set to work in 1339. When he left, Giovanni di Agostino and Domenico di Agostino carried on the work but meanwhile new events occured : Siena had suffered famine and hardships and in 1348 a terrible plague compelled her to give up her grandiose dream. Some errors, too, must have contributed to this decision as certain parts of the building had become dangerous and hed to be demolished; the apse was closed (1382) the vaults over the nave raised and the upper part of the facade, still unfinished, completed by Giovanni di Cecco to whose inspiration we owe also the Cathedral of Orvieto.

THE EXTERIOR

THE FACADE. - The graceful and imposing marble walls enlivened with alternate pink and black stripes, or rather dark green, are decorated with polychromic mosaics (fig. 18). This way of enlivening the dark marble is of Pisan origin and, earlier still, Oriental. The facade is the richest part of the building. According to the original concept the sculptural scheme was dedicated to the glorification of the Virgin to whom Siena devoted herself on the eve of the battle of Monteaperti. This is not so evident now because the statues are no longer ranged as they were at first; however, the lower part of the facade is dedicated to the Old Testament and the upper part to the New Testament; in the rose window is Virgin Mary.

The facade may be divided into two parts, the lower and the upper. The facade is thirty metres wide, forty-two metres high to the top of the central *Angel*, forty-six metres high to the top of the cupola. In 1410 the roof was covered with sheets of lead, the cupola with copper in 1698.

The lower part is the work of Giovanni Pisano and his pupils (1284-1296) amongst whom the well known Ramo di Paganello. It was completed in 1333 and is still a most vivid compendium of the earliest Italian Gothic sculpture. Of the three huge rectangular portals the central one is the highest; the arch over the central

STEFANO DI GIOVANNI detto IL SASSETTA
(Siena, 1392-1450)

Adorazione dei Magi (Palazzo Chigi Saracini)
Adoration des Mages (Palais Chigi Saracini)
The Wise Men in adoration (Palazzo Chigi Saracini)
Anbetung der heiligen drei Könige (Palazzo Chigi Saracini)

II.

portal is round, those over the side portals are pointed. Portals and arches are decorated with little columns, white and rose alternately, richly ornamented with spirals, foliage, flowers, cherubs, symbolic animals etc.; the capitals are ornamented with leaves. Carvings are in the lunettes and bas-reliefs in the spaces between the door and the architrave (in the centre), and between the architraves and the arches on the sides.

The central bas-relief represents the story of *Anne and Joachim* and is attributed to Tino di Camaino. On the architrave over the right portal is a Latin inscription commemorating the Jubilee proclaimed by Pope Boniface VIII in the year 1300. The lateral pillars continued in the upper part of the facade were designed by Giovanni Pisano but were modified during their execution.

Not all the statues are the work of Giovanni Pisano and his school, that is to say, of Agostino di Giovanni and Agnolo di Ventura.

During the repair works carried out in 1960 all the statues - even those on the sides - being damaged by time and exposure were placed in the Museum of the Cathedral (Museo dell'Opera Metropolitana) and copies were set up instead.

In the medallions on the spandrels are the busts of three Sienese Saints: from the left, Giovanni Colombini, Ambrogio Sansedoni and Andrea Gallerani, all by Tommaso Redi in the 17th. century.

The central bronze door was made by order of Count Umberto del Vescovo Sterbini, the Rector of the « Opera Metropolitana », with large contributions by the « Monte dei Paschi ». The coat-of-arms of both these institutions are seen in the frieze on the frame. It is a well planned harmonious work of art sculptured by Enrico Manfrini in 1958 illustrating the glorification of Virgin Mary by God and by Man (fig. 19).

The niches in the frieze running along the sides bare the figures of the women of the Old Testament (*Ruth, Judith, Esther* and *Anne*) of whom Mary is the representative, and the Prophets (*Isaiah, Michael, Jeremy* and *Solomon*) who predicted Mary's mission of misery and greatness. Up above are the Popes (Celestine I, Martin I, Pius IX and Pius X) who glorified Virgin Mary after her

Fig. 19 - The Cathedral. - The central door dedicated to the glorification of Virgin Mary, by Enrico Manfrini.

appearance on Earth. The central figures are those of *St. Bernardine* and *St. Catherine of Siena*, the protectors of the town. On the basis are eight episodes of the Virgin's life: *the Nativity, the Nuptials, the Annunciation, the Visitation, the Birth of Jesus, the Flight to Egypt, Cana's Nuptials, the Madonna at the Coenaculum.* Above these scenes are the large bas-reliefs representing *the Assumption* and the *Coronation of the Virgin.* The figures at the feet of the Madonna represent leading men in the fields of Religion, Poetry and Art summoned there to exalt the Virgin's glory; they are: *Raffaello, Sant'Alfonso de' Liguori, San Bonaventura, Sant'Ambrogio, Santa Teresa d'Avila, Michelangelo, San Bernardo, Duccio di Buoninsegna, Jacopo della Quercia, San Francesco d'Assisi, San Francesco di Sales,* the Archbishop of Siena *Mario Toccabelli, Blessed Angelico* and *Dante Alighieri.*

The upper part is separated from the lower by a cornice. It consists of three gables between two turrets which do not continue the line of the pillars in the lower central part .This is due to the fact that the upper part was built by Giovanni di Cecco in 1376 after the long lapse of time which had been dedicated to the building of the New Cathedral, according to a new design more consonant to the Gothic style, probably inspired by the Cathedral of Orvieto which is due to the Sienese Lorenzo Maitani.

This part of the facade, also, is richly decorated with friezes, statues and ornaments culminating in the great frame into which the rose window is inserted. The busts of thirty-six *Patriarchs* and *Prophets* are placed in little niches all around, on the top is the *Holy Virgin* and in the triangular sectors *the Four Evangelists* which are but copies of the originals, produced by Tito Sarrocchi and Leopoldo Maccari in the past century. The original statues are the work of the pupils of Giacomo di Bonfredi nicknamed Corbella (late 14th. century). The two lateral gables rest on a most elegant gallery of five pointed lobed arches. The central pillars, slim and graceful are crowned with pinnacles and statues. The mosaics in the gables were drawn by Luigi Mussini and Alessandro Franchi; they were made at Murano during the past century. On the left is *the Presentation of Mary;* in the middle, *the*

Coronation; on the right the *Crib.* On top of the highest pinnacle (72 metres) stands an Angel with outspread wings, the work of Tommaso Redi (1639).

THE SIDES are covered with alternate black and white stripes. The left side is grafted to the palace of the Archbishop and has but one blind single window, very high up. The right side reaches the walls of the unfinished New Cathedral. The four very fine blind double windows in the wall of the right aisle are the faithful reproduction of those of the Abbey of San Galgano; the double windows in the nave are also to be admired. Other five double windows are in the right wall of the cross where is the side door surmounted by a round basreliefs representing the *Madonna del Perdono* (the Madonna of Pardon) which is the work of Donatello (15th century).

The bronze door, called Chigiana door is the work of Vico Consorti and was offered to the Cathedral by Count Guido Chigi Saracini in 1946 as a thanksgiving to Virgin Mary, Patroness of Siena, for the salvation of the town during the last war.

THE STEEPLE. - Built over the foundations of an ancient tower belonging to the Bisdomini-Forteguerri family (1313) according to Agostino di Giovanni's and Agnolo di Ventura's designs it is decorated with horizontal black and white marble strips right to the very top. It is Romanesque, shaped after the Lombard-Pisan style with windows increasing from one single window at the bottom to sixfold windows at the top crowned with an octagonal spire with four pyramids in the corners. Behind the steeple rises the

CUPOLA. - A good view of it can be had from the right hand corner of the unfinished facade of the New Cathedral. It is hexagonal (1264) covered with ribbed tiles and surmonuted with a polygonal lantern. It rests on a drum round which run rows of galleries one on top of another (the well known Romanesque stylistic motif); the lower gallery is girded with slender acute arches resting on double columns whilst the arches encompassing the upper gallery are rounded.

THE HEAD OF THE CROSS. - Those who wish
to enjoy a full view of the perspective of the head of
the cross of the Cathedral (in the lower part almost
one Structure with the Baptistery which is the very
crypt of the Cathedral) should enter the right aisle
through the side door. The middle part of the walls is decorated with a series of little pointed arches; high up are
four single windows, and one below. The side portal in
the wall of the New Cathedral is most graceful and
elegant; it consists of a deep embrasure with a gable and
a lunette in which is a group of full-relief figures by
Giovanni d'Agostino in 1330.

Going back to the facade, on the pavement in front
of the portals are three graffiti, now restored, representing the cerimonies of the *Robing of the Ecclesiastical
Hierarchy*. Of the three portals only the right one is
usually open besides the portal in the side wall
caled Porta Chigiana. On the sides of the landing on
top of the steps in front of the Cathedral are two
columns each supporting a Sienese She-wolf suckling
twins. By the door on the right one enters the Cathedral.

THE INTERIOR

The interior is grandiose and austere, dominated by the
rhythm of the arches resting on dichromic columns (fig. 20).

The church is 89,52 metres long, 24,60 metres wide in
the nave, 51, 58 metres wide in the Latin cross; the nave
is 25,36 metres high and the aisles 16,30 metres.

The style is Romanesque, though not without some
touches of Gothic; the shape is that of a Latin cross with
one nave, two aisles a transept, apse and dome.

The nave is separated from the aisles by two rows of
five different styled pillars; the pillars continue in the
cross and reach the final vault; they are twentysix in all
Black and white horizontal marble stripes in equal succession cover the pillars in the nave; wide white horizontal
bands with narrow black stripes in the transept and in the
head of the cross. This decoration helps to restrain the

impression of uplift towards the vaults over the nave which are much higher than the lateral vaults, and it contributes light and colour to the whole building. The repetition creates a musical suggestion something like a « basso continuo » on which is elaborated the solemn architectural orchestration. The vaults over the transept are ribbed and painted blue with golden stars.

Many alterations were made as years went by in the planning and the decoration of the Cathedral. It began to assume its present aspect in 1506 when Pandolfo Petrucci ruled the town : then the presbitery which stood at first beneath the cupola was placed near the apse and lowered, all the lateral alters were modified, the precious old pictures were replaced with paintings by the best artists of the 17th. and 18th. centuries. Duccio di Buoninsegna's famous altar screen *La Maestà* was removed from the high altar and in its place a fine carved ciborium due to the master hand of Vecchietta was set up. (« Maestà » - Majesty - was the name given to the pictures of Virgin Mary and the Holy Child with Saints, Prophets and Patriarchs, from the 12th. to the 15th. century).

The special pride of the Cathedral of Siena, however, is the rare and most valuable floor. In 1372 some delightful graffiti began to be placed over the pre-existing brick floor in front of the high altar which at that time was under the cupola ; then they were continued down the nave. They are true works of art of polycromic marble. The painter used to send the drawings to the « maestri » (masters of stone) who prepared the marbles. The scenes and stories became ever more complex and perfect and took till 1562 to be completed. The whole, as is still visible, is a work of great beauty and mastery. Over forty artists worked at it through the years ; chronologically the first were the « Maestri Comacini » (a certain Marchese d'Adamo and his pupils) ; next came Sienese and Tuscan masters such as : Domenico di Niccolò de' Cori, Matteo di Giovanni, Bastiano di Francesco. Urbano da Cortona, Antonio Federighi, Paolo di Martino, Pietro del Minella, Neroccio di Bartolommeo Landi, Pinturicchio (from Umbria) and Beccafumi who was, no doubt, the best of them all ; he produced 35 biblical scenes. Many of the graffiti have been restored and some replaced with copies. We have no room here to describe each scene separately nor to speak of each author ; it will suffice to look at the following plant where the names of the most interesting scenes are written in capital letters.

THE FLOOR OF THE CATHEDRAL

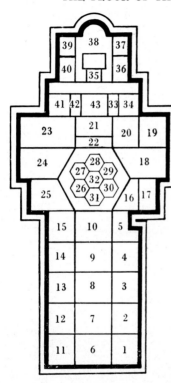

1. Urbano da Cortona - *Delphic Sibyl.*
2. Urbano da Cortona - *Cumaean Sibyl.*
3. Giovanni di Stefano - *Cumaean Sibyl.*
4. Antonio Federighi ERITHREAN SIBYL.
5. Urbano da Cortona - *Persian Sibyl.*
6. Giovanni di Stefano - *Hermes Trismegistus.*
7. (Modern copy of an original work made in 1373) - *Emblems of Siena and of her Allies.*
8. (Modern copy of the original made in 1373) - *Wheel with the Imperial Eagle.*
9. P. Mannucci. FORTUNE (after Pinturicchio's design)
10. (Modern copy) - *The wheel of Fortune.*
11. Guidoccio Cozzarelli - LYBIAN SIBYL.
12. Neroccio di Bartolommeo - *the Sibyl of the Hellespont.*
13. Urbano da Cortona - FRIGIAN SIBYL.
14. Matteo di Giovanni - SAMIAN SIBYL.
15. Benvenuto di Giovanni - ALBUNEAN SIBYL (fig. 23, page 78).
16. Antonio Federighi - *The Seven Ages of Man* (restored by Alessandro Franchi).
17. Domenico Beccafumi - *The three Theological Virtues and Religion.*

18. Bastiano di Francesco - *Victory of Jethro over the Ammonites.*
19. Pietro del Minella - *ABSALOM.*
20. Domenico di Bartolo - EMPEROR SIGISMOND.
21. Domenico Beccafumi - *Worshiping the Golden Calf.*
22. Domenico Beccafumi - *Moses drawing water from the Rock of Horeb.*
23. Antonio Federighi - JUDITH BEHEADING HOLOFERNES, AND THE BATTLE OF BETHANY.
24. Matteo di Giovanni - THE MASSACRE OF THE INNOCENTS.
25. Benvenuto di Giov. - HEROD BANISHED FROM THE TRONE.
26. Domenico Beccafumi - *The death of Ahab.*
27. Domenico Beccafumi - *Elijah's sacrifice;* (in the rhombs around): *Elijah tells Ardia to bring Ahab to him; Ardia taking Ahab to Elijah; Elijah fed by the ravens; Elijah annointing Jehu king of Israel; Elijah begging bread from the widow; Elijah resurrects the widow's son* (restored by Alessandro Franchi).
28. Domenico Beccafumi - THE SACRIFICE OF AHAB.
29. Domenico Beccafumi - *The Slaughter of the false Prophets of Baal.*
30. Domenico Beccafumi - *Elijah's reproach.*
31. Domenico Beccafumi - *Elijah ascends to Heaven.*
32. Domenico Beccafumi - *Agreement between Elijah and Ahab.*
33. Paolo di Martino - *Moses.*
34. Paolo di Martino - *Victory of Joshua over the Amorites.*
35. Domenico Beccafumi - ABRAHAM'S SACRIFICE.
36. Marchese d'Adamo and his Scholars - *Prudence.*
37. Marchese d'Adamo - *Temperance.*
38. Marchese d'Adamo - *Mercy.*
39. Marchese d'Adamo - *Justice.*
40. Marchese d'Adamo - *Fortitude.*
41. Paolo di Martino - *The victory of Samson over the Philistines.*
42. Domenico di Niccolò dei Cori - *Joshua.*
43. Domenico di Niccolò dei Cori - *David the Psalm singer with David with the sling, and the death of Goliath.*

The whole floor of the Cathedral is not visible all the year round; the oldest and most valuable graffiti are visible from August 15th. to September 15th. every year. However, in the Museum of the Cathedral are many drawings

Fig. 20 - The Cathedral - Inside view.

and reproductions which may be sufficient for a general idea of the whole.

Other characteristic features of the Cathedral are the 172 terracotta busts (often fanciful) of the first Popes, from Christ in the centre of the Apse with St. Peter on His left, all round the church up to Lucius III (1181-1185) on the right of Christ. These busts support little shelves on which rests the cornice beneath the vaults over the nave. Beneath the Popes are 36 busts of Emperors, from Constantine to Theodosius (15th. century).

Near the entrance, almost standing against the first pillars, on both sides are Antonio Federighi's finely wrought holy water stoups (1463).

The central door - The bas reliefs on the pedestals of the delightful, richly decorated columns on the sides of the door (the columns are the work of Giovanni di Stefano) represent scenes from the life of Virgin Mary; they are due to the master hand of Urbano da Cortona (1483) and come from the ancient altar of the Madonna delle Grazie. The very old bas-reliefs on the architrave were found near the Cathedral.

Rose window - The stained-glass represents the *Last supper*. Produced in 1549 by Pastorino dei Pastorini to Perin del Vaga's designs.

RIGHT AISLE.

On the facade, in a niche, stands the statue of *Paul V in the act of benedicting* (he was the Sienese Camillo Borghesi); this statue is the work of Fulvio Signorini (1605). The four altars resemble one another in style: they all have a veined marble plinth and columns with a spandrel. Just after the fourth altar is the Chigiana entrance door in the side wall of the church and next to it the door of the bell tower (from the top of which one may enjoy a good view of the whole region). Over this door is placed the simple but elegant tomb of Bishop Tommaso Piccolomini del Testa sculptured by Neroccio di Bartolommeo Landi in 1485. On the sides are marble frames containing bas-reliefs with scenes from *the life of Virgin Mary*. Remarkable is the scene representing *the Annunciation* due to Urbano da Cortona. By now the visitor is beneath the CUPOLA where once stood the presbitery; it is supported by six pillars (two pillars in the nave bear the flagpoles which, according to tradition, were on the « Carroccio » (charriot) at the battle of Monteaperti). The Cupola is decorated with painted cofferings; on the top is the lantern.

— 74 —

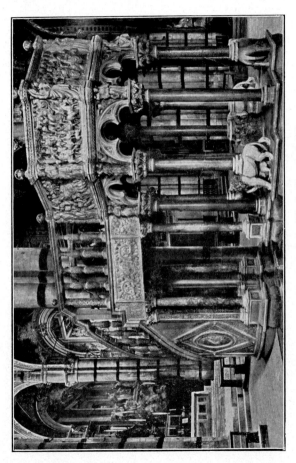

Fig. 21 - The Cathedral - *Nicola Pisano's Pulpit.*

In the six corners columns with fine capitals bear the gilt statues of the four *Sienese Patron Saints* and of *St. Catherine* and *St. Bernardine* modelled by Bastiano di Francesco and Ventura Turapilli in 1481. Above the statues are niches which divide the hexagon into a dodecagon in the drum. A blind gallery with forty-two columns runs all round the drum decorated in the spaces between the columns with chiaroscuro figures of *Patriarchs* and *Prophets* due to Guidoccio Cozzarelli, Benvenuto di Giovanni, Bastiano di Francesco and Pellegrino di Mariano (15th. century). Before visiting the right transept cross the space beneath the cupola right to the opposite side where is the finest piece of sculpture work treasured in the Cathedral: the marble PULPIT made by Nicola Pisano and his best pupils (his son Giovanni, Arnolfo di Cambio, Donato and Lapo Ciuccio di Ciuto in 1266-68; see fig. 21). This pulpit was completed by Nicola d'Apulia ten years after the pulpit in the Baptistery of Pisa and is a sample of the master's art when still influenced by his son Giovanni. The pulpit in the Cathedral of Pisa, with its thoughtful figures and the extreme simplicity of its perspective reveals a mature and genial assimilation of the highest classical ideals, that is to say, of the ideals of Romanesque art, but here this culminating point is surpassed and the influence of the Gothic style is already strongly felt. From the stylistic point of view this pulpit witnesses the transition from Romanesque art to Gothic art in sculpture. Pure Gothic are, in fact, the expression the grouping of the scenes, the complexity of the perspective planes. Here Nicola Pisano hardly shows any classical influence whatever, though such influences were then so strong in Pisa and plainly visible in all the statues and sarcofaghi of that Cathedral; here, he seeks nothing but the free expression of his own artistic personality.

At first the Pulpit was placed on the left side of the high altar right beneath the dome and rested directly on the floor like the pulpit in Pisa. When in 1506 the Presbitery was rebuilt to enlarge the Cathedral, it was removed to where it now stands (1543), a basement was placed under it and the marble staircase was added.

The Pulpit is octagonal; it rests on a marble basement upon which eight marble columns stand around a central column. On the left hand side, also supported by columns is the richly decorated marble casing of the elegant staircase designed by Riccio in 1570. The columns are alternately supported by four simple marble basements and four lions (two lionesses suckling their cubs and two lions devouring a young horse each). The central column stands on an octagonal basement and is supported by a group of eight marble figures : the *seven liberal Arts and Music*. All the lateral columns have Corinthian capitals and bear a section of the architrave on which are the figures of the *Sibyls*. Between the columns are trilobed arches with high-reliefs in the spandrels. The panels are seven, separated from one another by figures of *Prophets* and *Angels*. Proceding from the first panel just after the stairs, facing the left aisle they represent : 1) *The birth of Jesus and the Visitation*. 2) *The Arrival of the Magi and the Adoration of the Child*. 3) *The Presentation of Jesus in the Temple and the Flight to Egypt*. 4) *The Massacre of the Innocents*. 5) *the Crucifixion and the symbols of the Evangelists*. 6) *The last judgement of the Wicked*. 7) *The last judgment of the Elect*.

The narrative of the first two panels is serene and graceful but the rest, and above all the Crucifixion and the Judgment of the Wicked, accentuate the dramatic character of the scene : they are so intensely dramatic as to be considerd as presages of the mature art of Giovanni Pisano. On the parapet is perched an *eagle* which serves as a lectern.

Now let us visit the right arm of the cross

RIGHT TRANSEPT.

On the right is the CHAPEL OF THE MADONNA DEL VOTO otherwise called CAPPELLA CHIGI. It is Baroque, built in 1661 to the design of Benedetto Giovannelli by order of Pope Alexander VII (Fabio Chigi Saracini of Siena). It is circular, slightly eliptical with a drum and a gilt dome and is divided into eight panels by pillars in the lower part, buttresses in the drum and ribs on the dome. It contains works by Gian Lorenzo Bernini (1608-1680) the greatest Italian sculptor of the Baroque age. The altar is also his work but the delightful painted panel of the *Madonna del Voto*, seldom visible without permission, is ascribed to Guido da Siena (13th century). The *Tabernacle* and the gilt bronze *Angels* surrounding the panel of the Madonna are also the work of Bernini and so are the two marble statues in the niches just inside the door : *St. Jerome* and *St. Mary Magdalene*. The statue of *St. Catherine* and that of *St. Bernardine* on the sides of the altar are the work of two of Bernini's pupils : Ercole Ferrata and Antonio Raggi. The four panels between the columns with *scenes from the life of Mary* were made in Rome in 1748. On the left : *the Madonna visiting St. Elizabeth,* by Carlo Maratta (1625-1713) ; the opposite mosaic is the reproduction of another of Maratta's pictures : *the Holy Family resting in Egypt* which had to be removed because it was spoilt. Facing the altar is the bronze votive statue of *Gratitude* by Arturo Viligiardi (1918).

In the same arm of the cross are two other altars and two statues facing each other in niches: the statue on the right is *Pope Alexander III* (the Sienese Rolando Bandinelli) by Antonio Raggi 1663, on the left *Pope Alexander VII* by Ercole Ferrata (1668). In front of this statue is the tombstone of the *Sienese Bishop Carlo Bartoli* who died in 1444, by Federighi and by Giuliano da Como, designed by Del Minella. The altar in front of the tombstone is adorned with one of Mattia Preti's best compositions, probably made in 1650: *St. Bernardine preaching.* On the corner is the Cappella del Sacramento with a precious canvas by Alessandro Casolani: *Christmas* (1594) and a fine copper ciborium inlaid with malachite and lapislazzuli decorated with friezes and statues (made in Rome in 1742). On the right wall are five marble bas-reliefs by Giovanni di Turino: *the four Evangelists* and in the middle *St. Paul,* by Giovanni di Francesco da Imola.

Fig. 22 - The Cathedral - The Chapter Hall - Sano di Pietro: *St. Bernardine* (a detail).

Fig. 23 - The Cathedral - The floor - Benvenuto di Giovanni: *The Albunean Sibyl.*

Fig. 24 - The Cathedral - Tino di Camaino - *Cardinal Petroni's monument*: St. Paul.

THE PRESBITERY.

Three steps lead to it with a grating in the middle through which one can look down into the Baptistery below

THE HIGH ALTAR is the work of Pellegrino di Pietro (1536). It is surmounted with a bronze ciborium that weighs 748 kg. made by Vecchietta in 1467-72 : the whole is the conception of Baldassarre Peruzzi. The Angels bearing candelabra placed high up are the work of Giovanni di Stefano (1489), those placed lower down, of Francesco di Giorgio Martini (1499). The eight candelabra in the shape of angels standing on the ledges of the pillars in the nave are by Beccafumi (1550). On the right hand side of the altar is the « residenza » *in cornu epistolae,* a long chest finely carved by Benedetto di Giovanni and Domenico di Filippo, designed by Riccio in 1575. Most remarkable for gracefulness and liveliness are the twenty-two statues of *Angels* and *Virtues* on the lid. On the left hand side of the altar is the Episcopal Throne made by Tito Corsini in 1907 according to some designs of Riccio's. High up on the opposite walls two orchestra galleries face each other ; the one on the right wall is the work of Antonio Barili and of his nephew Giovanni with the help of Giovanni di Pietro called Castelnuovo (1510) ; the one on the left wall was designed by Riccio and carved by Lorenzo di Bartolomeo da Lucca in 1550.

THE APSE.

A splendid set of wooden stalls is in the apse ; they are 51, very finely carved. This part of the Chancel is Renaissance work and was sculptured in 1567-1570 by Benvenuto di Giovanni and Teseo di Bartolino who drew inspiration from Riccio. The few stalls on the side walls show Gothic influences ; they were carved by several clever artists under the direction of Francesco del Tonghio in 1362-1397. The very fine carvings on the lateral parts of the chancel come from the Monastery of « Monteoliveto Maggiore » and are the work of Frate Giovanni da Verona (1503). This Monastery was at first known as Monteoliveto Minore and became famous because Blessed Bernardo Tolomei — the founder of the Order — died there in 1348. In spite of the fact that two styles of work chronologically so different are placed side by side, the whole is fine and rich and quite organic. The delightful lectern was made by Benedetto di Giovanni and Domenico di Filippo in 1558 ; by Beccafumi in 1544 are the restored figures of the Apostles still to be seen beside

AENEAS·FEDERICO·III·IMP·LEONORAM·SP[...]
EXHIBET·ET·PVELLAE·LAVDIS·AC·REG[...]
LVSITANORVM·COMPLE[...]

BERNARDINO DI BETTO detto IL PINTURICCHIO
(Perugia, 1454-1518)

Incontro di Eleonora di Portogallo con Federico III a Siena
(Cattedrale)
Rencontre d'Eléonore de Portugal avec Frédéric III à Sienne
(Cathédrale)
Meeting of Eleonor of Portugal with Frederick III in Siena
(Cathedral)
Begegnung der Eleonora von Portugal mit Friedrich III in Siena (Kathedrale)

III.

Bartolomeo Cesi's splendid canvas of *the Assumption* (1594). On the upper part of the wall is painted *Trinity in Glory* (1812) by that same Francesco Mazzuoli who restored some of the pre-existing figures frescoed by Beccafumi. On the sides of the Apse (on the right) are the figures of *Esther and Ahasuerus* and many *Sienese* Saints; on the left side of the apse we see the *Jews in the Desert* and the figures of other *Sienese Saints,* all due to Ventura Salimbeni (1608-1611).

The stained glass window in the head of the cross was made by the Sienese masters Dono and Giunta di Paolo according to the cartoons purposely drawn by Duccio di Buoninsegna. In 1369 some parts were re-painted by Giacomo da Castello. On the left of the Presbitery is the Sacristy.

THE SACRISTY

contains many precious works of art but can be visited only by request. Most remarkable is a white marble holy water stoup decorated with coloured enamels and gilt bronze, one of Giovanni di Turino's most exquisite jewellery masterpieces. There is also a good bronze bust of *Alexsander VII* due to Bernini. In the *Chapter Room* are three of Sano di Pietro's panels : *A Portrait of St. Bernardine* (fig. 22), *St. Bernardine preaching in the Campo square* (1430) and *in Piazza San Francesco* (1440) all most interesting because of the architecture of the houses and squares (the Town Hall is only one storey high, as in fact it was in those early times).

LEFT TRANSEPT

In the corner Chapel dedicated to S. Ansano (right opposite the Chapel of the Sacrament) is an interesting canvas representing *Sant'Ansano baptizing the Sienese,* by Francesco Vanni in 1596. On the floor is a bronze basrelief covering the tomb of *Bishop Pecci,* produced by Donatello in 1426 (it is generally covered up ; to see it, call the door keeper). Over the altar is the masterpiece which, for beauty, ranks with Nicola Pisano's Pulpit : CARDINAL RICCARDO PETRONI'S SEPULCRHAL MONUMENT. It is a grandious Gothic piece of sculpture by Tino di Camaino and his father Camaino di Crescentino in 1314-18. Cardinal Petroni was one of the most learned men and famous jurists of his age who died in 1314. This monument was composed as it actually is in 1951 ; it consists of a basement with shelves on which four youthful caryatides stand in thoughtful attitudes uphold-

Fig. 25 - The Cathedral - The Piccolomini Library - Pinturicchio:
E. S. Piccolomini crowned a Poet by Frederick III.

ing the sarcophagus adorned with full-reliefs and bas-reliefs, as follows : (in the middle) *Christ Risen;* in the right : *St. Thomas's Incredulity;* on the left : *The Apparition of Mary Magdalene.* On the lid of the sarcophagus is the catafalque on which rests the statue of the Cardinal beneath a curtain upheld by two Angels. The whole is surmounted with three exquisite Gothic gables in which are placed the statues of the *Madonna and Holy Child* (in the middle), of *St. Peter* and *St. Paul* on the sides (see fig. 24).

Near the large hexagon under the cupola stands Nicola Pisano's pulpit, described at page 76.

Next come two statues in opposite niches (on the right *Pius II,* by Giuseppe Mazzuoli in 1698; on the left, *Pius III* by Pietro Balestra in 1706) and two altars ranged in symmetrical order with those in the right transept. The left altar has a good wooden *Crucifix* which is said to have been on the Chariot of the Republic at the battle of Monteaperti ; it is a 14th. century work. On the floor is a good graffito tombstone. Next comes the CHAPEL OF ST. JOHN THE BAPTIST. It is the work of Giovanni di Stefano ; built right opposite the Cappella del Voto it has the same shape though the style is that of the Renaissance. Marrina's marble portal richly decorated with friezes and bas-reliefs has on each side two columns one above the other. The two lower ones stand on pedestals (ornamented with festoons, figures and symbolic animals) which are said to have belonged to a Roman altar ; now however they are generally attributed to Antonio Federighi. The iron gate is the work of Sallustio di Francesco Barili. In this Chapel St. John the Baptist's right arm is treasured inside a reliquary which is shown to the people only on St. John's day. It was presented by Tomaso Paleologo to Pope Pius II who gave it to Siena in the year 1464. In the middle of the Chapel is placed the Baptismal Font ascribed to Antonio Federighi ; it is octagonal, decorated with a series of bas reliefs representing *six stories about Adam and Eve, Samson and the Lion, Hercules and the Centaur.* In the central niche is the bronze statue of *St. John the Baptist,* by Donatello (1457), which is rather unfinished from the artistic point of view but most vigorous and expressive. In the niche on the right is the statue of *St. Catherine of Alexandria* sculptured by Neroccio di Bartolommeo Landi in 1487 ; in the left niche is *Sant'Ansano* by Giovanni di Stefano in 1487. The frescoes in the eight sectors were painted by Pinturicchio in 1501-1504. Only five of them are still as they originally were as three were restored in 1608 by Francesco Rustici called Rustichino. Of these three, one was replaced in 1868 with another painting by Cesare Maccari because it had suffered damage. On the lower part of the wall, from the left: *Alberto Aringhieri the Rector of the Works of the Cathedral as a young man in the robes of a Knight of Malta* by Pinturicchio; *the Birth of the Baptist,* by Pinturicchio; on the right: *Francesco Aringhieri as an old man in civilian dress,* by Pinturicchio; a statue of *the Beheading of the Baptist,* by Rustici. On the upper part of the wall, on the left: *the Baptist in the Desert,* by Pinturicchio and *the Baptism of Jesus Christ,* by Rustici; on the right: *St. John preaching,* by Pinturicchio; *St. John in Prison,* by Cesare Maccari. In a niche on the side wall near the entrance is the statue of *the Sienese Marcantonio Zondadari,* by Giuseppe Mazzuoli and his nephew Bartolomeo in 1725.

LEFT AISLE

Under the first vault is the monumental marble entrance to the PICCOLOMINI LIBRARY. It has two huge exquisitely ornamented arches produced by Marrina in 1497. Under the right arch is an altar with a very precious basrelief by Vecchietta representing *St. John the Evangelist;* under the left arch is the bronze gate which closes the entrance to the Library, produced by Antonio Ormanni in 1497. In the lunette is a huge fresco painted by Pinturicchio to illustrate *the Coronation of Pius III.* The Library was built by order of Cardinal Francesco Todeschini Piccolomini (Pope Pius III) in 1495 to honour his maternal uncle Pope Pius II (1458-1464) and house his books.

It is a large rectangular room, well lighted and brightly decorated with Pinturicchio's splendid frescoes which are still in a perfect state. In the middle of the vault is the coat-of-arms of the Piccolomini family, around it are allegorical and mythological scenes painted by the Master's pupils; remarkable are the grottesques beneath the painted arches and spandrels. The whole ceiling, so bright and full of decorative fantasy is a feast for the eyes. The floor is made of majolica tiles with the emblems of the Piccolomini family. On the wooden shelves carved by Antonio Barili in 1496 are treasured miniated chorals some of which are worthy of attention and praise owing to the skill and beauty of the decorations, especially those produced by Liberale da Verona and Girolamo da Cremona. Among the Sienese miniaturists, worthy of praise are Sano di Pietro, Pellegrino di Mariano, Guidoccio Cozzarelli and Benvenuto di Giovanni.

On the walls, in the spaces between the painted arches are Pinturicchio's splendid brillant coloured frescoes which date back to 1505-1507. They illustrate the life of Enea Silvio Piccolomini (1405-1464) the Archbishop of Siena, later on Pope Pius II who was one of the noblest popes of the Renaissance. They are ten and start at the bottom of the room near the window on the right hand side of the entrance door. The first fresco is : 1) *Young Piccolomini starting for the Council of Basle;* 2) *He acts as the Council's Ambassador at the Court of King James of Scotland;* 3) *Emperor Frederick III crowns him with a Poet's garland* (fig. 25); 4) *Frederick III sends him as Ambassador to Pope Eugenius IV;* 5) *As Bishop of Siena he presents Eleonora of Portugal to her betrothed Frederick III, at Porta Camolia;* 6) *Pope Callistus III elects him Cardinal;* 7) *He ascends the Pontifical Throne;* 8) *At Mantoa he stands for the Crusade against the Turks;* 9) *He proclaims the Canonization of St. Catherine of Siena;* 10) *at Ancona preparing the expedition against the Turks.* Of the whole set of frescoes the fifth and the sixth are generally considered the best. Over the entrace door is placed a fine stucco bas-relief representing *the Expulsion of Adam and Eve from Earthly Paradise,* ascribed to Jacopo della Quercia.

Proceding along the left aisle we find Bandino Bandini's monument with a group by some follower of Michelangelo's in the 16th. century representing *Christ Risen between Angels;* next to it is the grandiose PICCOLOMINI ALTAR by Andrea Bregno (1481-1485). In the niches are the statues of *St. Gregory, St. Paul, St. Peter* and *St. Pius,* all by Michelangelo who started also the statue of *St. Francis,* later on finished off by Torrigiani. The *Madonna* in the niche above has recently been ascribed to the early art of Jacopo della Quercia. A most remarkable work of art is the *Nursing Madonna* in a marble frame, very likely by Paolo di Giovanni Fei (1381). Next come three altars like the opposite ones in the right aisle. Standing against the facade is the statue of *Pope Marcellus II* (the Sienese Marcello Cervini), by Domenico Cafaggi in 1593.

Coming out of the Cathedral and turning to the left we enjoy the view of the superb remnants of the NEW CATHEDRAL which, should have covered the whole vast rectangular square with the long arm of its cross. The right aisle spanned by five huge round arches with one single window on the outside facade is grafted to the Cathedral; within the spaces beneath three of the arches is now ranged the Museum of the Cathedral. On the opposite wall are other three single windows, now blind as they are now blocked up by the wall of the Palazzo della Prefettura. At the bottom of the square stands the huge unfinished facade called « IL FACCIATONE ». Looking at these architectural remains it is easy to understand how beautiful and imposing the whole building should have been if the new part of the Cathedral had been completed (fig. 17, page 61).

THE MUSEUM OF THE CATHEDRAL
(Museo dell'Opera Metropolitana)

Contains a most interesting collection of the works of art produced for the Cathedral and was started in 1870.

GROUND FLOOR.

This large room is divided into two unequal parts by a 15th. century wrought iron gate which was formerly in the Hospital of Santa Maria della Scala together with the marble

Fig. 26 - The Museum of the Cathedral - Giovanni Pisano: *Mary the daughter of Moses.*

Fig. 27 - The Museum of the Cathedral - *The Three Graces* (copy of a 3rd century work).

staircase leading to the upper rooms. Only sculpture works are gathered here and chiefly those by Giovanni Pisano and his school. Before the gate are : the front of a Roman sarcophagus decorated with *Tritons and Nereids;* a statue of *St. Peter* and a spire belonging to the facade of the Cathedral, a few panels representing : the *Annunciation* by Urbano da Cortona, the *Church and symbols of the Evangelists* by Arnolfo di Cambio, Bartolomeo da Cortona's portrait of *St. Bernardine of Siena* and a *Head by* Giovanni di Agostino. Then comes another *spire* from the facade, another statue of St. Peter by Urbano da Cortona and that of a Saint by Giovanni di Agostino. Near the gate are placed some marble capitals of Nicola Pisano's scool, probably meant for the old chancel of the Cathedral.

Beyond the gate, on a 15th. century pedestal probably due to Federighi, are the *Three Graces* (fig. 27). It is a roman copy of the original belonging to the school of Praxitiles, produced in the 3rd. century ; the harmony and elegance of the whole composition accounts for the admiration and praise it enjoys (it has been imitated by Pinturicchio and also by Canova). On the sides of the room are some sculptures made for the facade of the Cathedral, actually replaced with very fine copies, and a collection of statues, also produced for the Cathedral, which rank among the best in Italan Gothic art. Near the gate are two marble she-wolves (14th. and 16th. centuries) and the statues of two angels ascribed to Giovanni di Agostino. The six statues along the left wall with the symbols of the Evangelists (two lions, a horse and a bull) are : *Moses, Mary the daughter of Moses* (mark her sweet expression ; fig. 26), *Simeon, Sibyl,* Giovanni Pisano's *Isaiah* and *a Saint,* probably *Luke,* by Camaino di Crescentino. Other eleven statues are ranged against the right wall, all by Giovanni Pisano : the second is *Solomon, Giosuè* the third - *Plato* the fourth - *a Prophet,* the fifth - *Abacuc,* the sixth - *Aristotle,* the senventh - *David,* the eighth - *Balaam,* the tenth. After the statues come two tabernacles with *St. Mathew and St. Luke* on the front, by Tino di Camaino, and on the back *two figures* by Giovanni di Cecco. Over the 16th century altar is *the Baptism of Jesus,* by Andrea and Raffaello Piccinelli nicknamed Brescianini in 1524. These two artists show the influence of Andrea del Sarto. On the floor are some old marble graffiti from the floor of the Cathedral representing the *Six Ages of Man,* by Antonio Federighi in 1475 ; the marble slab is supposed to be Tommaso Pecci's tombstone ascribed to Tino di Camaino. The four panels represent the *Annunciation,* the *Nativity,* the *Adoration* and the *Wise Men offering gifts.*

The ARCHIVES can be visited only by special leave. They contain reproductions, letters, documents, autographs and papers concerning the building of the Cathedral.

THE FIRST FLOOR

THE HALL OF DUCCIO. This hall is supplied with a very modern system of air conditioning and illumination. Since January 28th. 1961 it has become the seat of the greatest masterpiece of the Sienese school « *La Maestà* » (Majesty). The front panel was restored at the "Istituto centrale del Restauro in Rome from 1953 to 1957; the back panel from 1957 to 1959. It was painted by Duccio di Buoninsegna as an altar screen for the High Altar of the Cathedral and placed there in 1311. The admiration and happiness of the people were such that public manifestations of joy took place in the streets while the picture was being carried from the painter's house (see p. 131) to the Cathedral. It had steps and gables and was painted on both sides with 60 pictures of the life of *Jesus and Mary,* 16 of which were on the side turned towards the people with 7 figures of prophets and 10 busts of Apostles; 44 pictures were on the back side of the panel. This picture was in the Cathedral till 1505. In 1771 the two panels were separated and placed one in the Chapel of the Sacrament and the other in the Chapel of Sant'Ansano (still in the Cathedral) and the steps and gables, being no longer useful, were removed. (At present 10 panels are abroad : 3 in the National Gallery in London, 4 in Washington, 2 in the Rockfeller Collection and 1 in the Frick Collection-New Sork. Six are lost).

On the left side of the entrance is the panel that used to face the Chancel; it is divided into 26 pictures which tell the story of the life of Jesus *(The entrance to Jerusalem, The Washing of the Feet, the Last Supper, the Speech after the Supper, Judah's agreement, the Prayer in the Orchard, Jesus arrested, the First Abjuration, Christ and Anne, Christ and Caiaphas, Christ beaten, Christ at the Praetorium, Pilate's interrogation, Christ and Herod, Christ led back to Pilate, the Flagellation, the crown of Thorns, Pilate washes his hands, the Calvary, the Crucifixion, the Deposition, the Burial, the Maries et the Sepulchre, Descent to Limbo, Apparition to Magdalene, Apparition to Emaus.*

Right opposite the entrance is the part of the picture that used to face the people (fig. 28). In the middle sits the Madonna on a rich romanesque throne on the base of which is the inscription : Mater *Sancta Dei sis causa Senis requiei - sis Ducio vita te quia pinxit ita.* (Holy Mother of God. bestow peace on Siena, and salvation on Duccio who painted thee). The Holy Child is sitting on her lap and around them are 20 Angels and Saints. Kneeling in front of the Madonna are the Patron Saints of Siena : *Sant'Ansano, San Savino, San Crescenzio and San Vittore*. Beneath the little arches in the upper part of the panel are painted the figures of 10 Apostles. Many of the pieces belonging to the steps and basement are to be seen along the left wall of the room. The central part of the picture and even the smaller panels, to the production of which many of Duccio's pupils are said to have worked, are quite enough to afford a general idea of the original beauty of this delightful altar screen. The central part where the Madonna is seated on the throne still shows Byzantine influences in the simmetry of the figures, their full-face position and in the gold backround, but they are nothing more than traces as the faces, even though slightly slanting and motionless, have an expression of their own which is very far from the hieratic expression of the Oriental Theophanies. ; the colours are no longer spread over large surfaces with the same intensity but are enriched with carefully sought variations. The admirable panels representing the *Massacre of the Innocents, the Flight to Egypt, the Temptation in the Temple, the Annunciation, St. Thomas's incredulity, the Miraculous fishing* show in a most unexpected and sudden manner, so soon after the Byzantine way of painting, the world of man and all the variety of human feelings placed within Nature herself. The pictorial qualities of the panels bring to evidence the value of the forms no longer as a mere abstract and decorative element as it was with the Byzantines but as the representation of movement, with an expression and spirit of their own. From this altar screen Simone Martini drew inspiration for his *"Maestà"* (see page 44).

On the same left wall is the triptych of the *Nativity of Mary* by Pietro Lorenzetti, dated 1342. This admirable painting was imitated by Paolo di Giovanni Fei (now in the Picture Gallery ; see page 106). The equilibrium between the figures and the architecture is perfect. Remark the details of the clothes and of the fan, in particular.

In the same room is also the *Madonna and Child* known as the *Madonna di Crevole* because once it was in the Church of Santa Cecilia at Crevole ; it is ascribed to Duccio during the early years of his life.

Outside the room, on the landing is the terracotta bust of *Bartolomeo Carosi,* otherwise Brandano or the Madman of Christ, by an anonymous artist of the 16th. century.

THE SECOND FLOOR.

This large room is full of the remnants of the Treasury of the Cathedral and of the Hospital of Santa Maria della Scala. From the left, a 16th. century embroidered *altar screen* formerly in the Church of the Hospital of Santa Maria della Scala. In the first glass case : ostensories among which Pope Pius X's (Papa Sarto) decorated with the symbols of the Evangelists. The polychrome terracotta representing *St. John the Evangelist* is a 16th century work by Guidoccio Cozzarelli. In the second glass case : sacred vestments from the sacresty of the Cathedral. In the third : some 14th. century ivory pastoral staffs and the urn made by Francesco d'Antonio in 1465 for St. John the Baptist's arm. In the fourth : the gold rose donated by Pope Alexandre VII in 1658 and some vestments from the Cappella del Voto. In the fifth : some relics and the terracotta model made by Gian Lorenzo Bernini for his *San Girolamo,* now in the Cappella del Voto (in the Cathedral). In the sixth : the painted wooden statues of *four Sienese Saints* (Sant'Ansano, San Crescenzio, San Savino and San Vittore) by Francesco di Valdambrino in the 15th century, a painted wooden Crucifix of the 15th. century and a polychrome statue of St. Paul by Guido del Tonghio. In the seventh : the twelve wooden statues of the *Apostles* made by Giuseppe Mazzuoli - the best of Bernini's followers - as models for the marble statues once on the facade of the Cathedral. They were pulled down in the past century and are now in Bromton Oratory, London.

In the adjoining smaller hall see the polychrome wooden statue of San Savino by Guido del Tonghio in the 14th. century ; a silver and gold altar screen by some 17th. century Roman goldsmiths ; *Christ bearing the Cross* by Domenico Beccafumi ; a 16th. century *Madonna* ascribed to Francesco di Giorgio Martini ; Vecchietta's 15th. century fresco of the « Pietà » ; *a Madonna with the Holy Babe* by Ambrogio di Baldese and , in the middle of the room, the *Reliquary* made for the *head of San Galgano* in the 13th. century. This admirable Gothic piece of art is of great importance for the study of the works produced by the Sienese goldsmiths.

On the staircase is a bronze statue of *Christ Risen* by Fulvio Signorini in 1595 and on the wall a 15th. century fresco of *Christ crucified,* Now go up to the

THIRD FLOOR.

The large hall contains some very interesting works of art of the Sienese school ; remarkable is the Madonna known as *The large eyed Madonna* (la Madonna dagli occhi grossi) by an anonymous Sienese painter of the 13th. century. It was made for the high alter of the Cathedral before Duccio's « Maestà » was placed there ; then it was placed in the Chapel of the Madonna del Voto where it was left till

Fig. 28 - The Museum of the Cathedral - Duccio di Buoninsegna : « *Maestà* » (the front panel)

the 17th. century. It is important for the study of early Sienese painting and historically because it was in front of this Madonna that the Sienese knelt in prayer before the battle of Monteaperti and, in later years, offered the town to Virgin Mary. Next comes Gualtieri di Giovanni's *Crucifixion;* the doors of an old reliquary decorated inside with scenes of the *Construction and Raising of the Cross,* by Benedetto di Bindo and Giovanni di Bindino di Cialli in 1412; beneath these scenes are *Prophets, Angels and Saints,* also painted in 1412 by Benedetto di Bindo and his pupils. Then comes *St. Jerome* by Giovanni di Paolo, and in the gables *the Redeemer.* Next, four panels (once belonging to a many panelled picture) with the figures of *Saints* by Ambrogio Lorenzetti, in the gables there are other figures of *Saints* by the same author; *the Articles of the Creed* by Nicola di Nardo in 1412; a delightful fragment of a panelled picture with *the Madonna suckling the Holy Babe among Saints,* signed Gregorio di Cecco di Luca and dated 1423. A Panel once belonging to some altar piece representing *St. Francis appearing to St. Anthony in the Chapter of Arles,* by Giovanni di Paolo dated 1440-1445. It is a delightful scene: St. Francis is blessing the Friars assembled in front of St. Anthony, some bewildered, some perplexed and others in attitude of penitence; beyond the three-fold windows in the background a smiling blue sky crowns the scene. Last comes Sano di Pietro's *Madonna and Holy Babe.* Against the opposite wall stands a 15th. century decorated and painted wedding coffer.

On the way back, on the left is the hall called SALONCINO DI VITTORIO ALFIERI because here the poet interpreted his own tragedies in 1777 (see the inscription). On the walls are the following pictures: an altar screen with the figure of *St. Paul* by Domenico Beccafumi in the 16th. century; an organ door with *Angels singing* by Girolamo Mogagni in 1515; an altar screen with the *Madonna and Saints* by Cristoforo Roncalli, nicknamed Pomarancio in 1576; a bierhead with the *Madonna and Holy Babe and a Saint* by Raffaello Vanni in 1608; another altar screen with *an Enthroned Madonna between St. Bernardine and St. Anthony of Padua* by Matteo di Giovanni in 1460 and some altar steps (or basement) with a delightful *Madonna and Child among Angels and Saints* by the same author in 1479; a lunette with *Angels* by G.B. Giusti in 1630; a side panel with *Saint Anthony of Padua* by Matteo Balducci in the 16th. century; *Christ in front of Pilate* and the *Deposition* by Luca Giordano in the 17th. century; *the Madonna and St. Anthony* by some artist of Beccafumi's school. In the middle of the room there are two glass cases containing 13th. century miniated chorals which are very important to the history of the Sienese miniatures.

The next room is hung with red and gold velvet (17th. century). Treasured inside glass cases are several altar screens, and sacred vestments worthy of praise.

Through the little door at the bottom of the room one may reach the FACCIATONE (facade) of the new Cathedral. Two bas-reliefs are on the landing at the top of the first flight of steps : the *Madonna and Holy Child* and *Christ between two Cherubins,* both the work of Giovanni d'Agostino in 1345. At the top of the stairs may be enjoyed one of the most beautiful views of the town and surroundings.

Right opposite the facade of the Cathedral is the long prospect of

THE HOSPITAL OF SANTA MARIA DELLA SCALA
(Ospedale di Santa Maria della Scala)

According to tradition this Hospital was founded in the year 832 by Beato Sorore, a Sienese cobbler. The building as we actually see it was started in the 13th. century by the Canons of the Cathedral; its original stylistic character is still to be seen in the elegant double windows. It was called « della Scala » (of the stairway) because it is situated opposite the stairway of the Cathedral (the coat-of-arms of the Hospital, in fact, bears a ladder surmounted with a cross). Wishing to visit the Hospital one may enter any day from 12,30 to 1,30 p.m.; in other hours, apply to the door keeper.

The First Vestible. On the left is the tomb of Jacopo Tondi, by G. Cozzarelli in 1507; the Renaissance ceiling is the work of Guidoccio d'Andrea. *The Second Vestible* : a fresco representing the *Encounter of Ann and Joachim,* by Beccafumi in 1512. THE PILGRIMS' HALL (now occupied by the sick) is decorated with a rare and most interesting cycle of frescoes of the 15th. century illustrating the vicissitudes of the Hospital and the calling of nursing the sick and the poor and above all the orphans. The colours are bright and the scenes awake our interest because they show the costumes and architecture of that time. Some of these paintings, however, are badly damaged. Facing the entrance door looking to the left where the windows are we see the following scenes. By Domenico di Bartolo in 1440-43 : 1) *Episodes of Charity;* 2) *The Re-*

ception and Marriage of the Orphans; 3) *The Distribution of Alms;* 4) *The Care of the sick.* By Giovanni Novesi in 1507 : *the Wet Nurses receive the Infants and their wages.* On the opposite wall, going from the window towards the bottom of the room: 1) By Pietro d'Achille Crogi in the 16th. century, *the Nurses receive wheat as their wages* (this scene is badly damaged); 2) *Celestinus II granting Autonomy to the Hospital,* by Domenico di Bartolo in 1433; 3) *Blessed Agostino Novello robes the Rector of the Hospital,* by Priamo della Quercia, Jacopo's brother, in 1432; 4) *the Enlargement of the Hospital,* by Domenico di Bartolo (this scene is most interesting for the details of the architecture); 5) *the Foundlings ascending to Heaven,* by Lorenzo di Pietro nicknamed Vecchietta in 1441.

In the Library, which is generally closed, are other frescoes painted by Vecchietta in the lapse of time from 1446 to 1449; they represent *scenes from the Old Testament* but are badly damaged. There is also a fine Madonna called *Madonna of Mercy* painted by Domenico di Bartolo in 1444 and in the Infirmary of St. Pius the portrait of *Blessed Sorore,* a monochrome painting ascribed to Domenico di Bartolo. In many other wards of the Hospital are some good but not excellent frescoes.

Adjoining the Vestibule is the CHURCH OF SANTA MARIA DELLA SCALA otherwise called of SS. ANNUNZIATA, founded in 1252 but completed as we actually see it in the year 1466 by Guidoccio d'Andrea. It has but one rectangular nave and a good wooden coffered ceiling with painted decorations. Most interesting are the two fine carved choir galleries, richly decorated and ornamented; the one on the right hand side is ascribed to Baldassarre Peruzzi. On the altar is a bronze statue of *Christ Risen,* the work of Vecchietta in the year 1476. In the Chancel is a bright and happy fresco representing the *Pool of Bethel* painted by Sebastiano Conca in 1732. The wooden stalls in the chancel were carved by Ventura Turapilli in 1490.

Just outside the Church of SS. Annunziata on the right is the portal that leads to ST. CATHERINE'S ORATORY beneath the vaults of the Hospital, called DELLA NOTTE - of the night - (18th. c. stucco work). Here is the cell in which Catherine Benincasa used to rest after having tended the sick in the Pilgrims' Hall. There is a good terracotta portrait of the *Saint asleep,* made by Vecchietta in 1641. In the Sacristy is a triptych by Taddeo di Bartolo in 1400 re-

Fig. 29 - The Baptistery - *The Facade*.

presenting the *Madonna seated on a throne with St. John the Baptist and St. Andrew;* four heads of beirs ascribed to Matteo Balducci (the last years of the 16th. century). On the altar is a sculptured *Madonna and Holy Child* of Giovanni Pisano's school belonging to the 14th. century, and oil paintings by Rutilio Manetti and Francesco Rustici.

Adjoining the Oratory is the CONFRATERNITY OF THE DISCIPLINED, once a catacomb called the *Devoted Cave of the Flagellants*, now the seat of the Executors of Pious Dispositions. On the altar of the Oratory is a *Madonna and Saints* by A. Casolani. In the Sacristy : *the Last Judgement*, of the school of the Lorenzetti brothers; *Saint John the Baptist*, by Giovanni di Paolo; in a lunette « *Pietà* » by Sano di Pietro. There is also the *Holy Family*, painted by Sodoma in 1520 and other works.

Returning to the Piazza, on the left hand side stands the PALAZZO GRANDUCALE o DELLA PREFETTURA (the Grand-Ducal Palace) started in 1489 by Giacomo Petrucci the brother of Pandolfo but enlarged and embellished after the Baroque style towards the end of the 16th. century to Bernardo Buontalenti's design; these works were ordered by the Medici who established in this palace their official residence as Governors On the left is the PALACE OF THE ARCHBISHOP which is grafted to the Cathedral. The facade is gothic decorated with black and white bands. It dates back to the years from 1718 to 1723. It contains a Chapel with the picture of *San Biagio* by Riccio and, in a gold frame, Ambrogio Lorenzetti's *Madonna del Latte (Nursing Madonna)* which is generally accepted as his masterpiece (fig. 51). The colours are remarkably fresh and the scene extremely human. Low down on the side is a Latin inscription in Lombard letters commemorating the spot where Giovanni Pisano chose to be buried.

[At the bottom of the « Vicolo di S. Girolamo » in Via dei Fusari is the CHURCH of SAN SEBASTIANO IN VALLE PIATTA, otherwise called the ROTONDA DEGLI INNOCENTI, which belongs to the Contrada della Selva (Forest); once it was the Monastery of the « Gesuate » called « povere di Vallepiatta » (1367). It was built by Domenico Ponsi to Baldassarre Peruzzi's design in 1507. It is in Renaissance style and has a pretty cylindrical dome. Inside it has the shape of a Greek Cross

DUCCIO DI BUONINSEGNA (Siena, 1260-1319)

Pilato si lava le mani : particolare del tergo della *Maestà*
(Museo della Cattedrale)
Pilate se lave les mains : détail du verso de la *Majesté*
(Musée de la Cathédrale)
Pilate washes his hands : part of the rear of *Majesty*
(Cathedral Museum)
Pilatus wäscht seine Hände : Ausschnitt-Rückseite der
Maestà (Museum der Kathedrale)

IV.

with harmonious decorations produced in the 16th. and 17th. centuries. Il contains the following works of art: the *Adoration of the Magi,* by Astolfo Petrazzi; the *Crucifixion,* by Rutilio Manetti; *Madonna with Saints,* by Guidoccio Cozzarelli; the *Madonna and Saints* by Benvenuto di Giovanni; a precious reliquary made in the year 1379 and many trophies of the Palio].

After having visited Piazza del Duomo the visitor should walk through the arch way of the Duomo Nuovo (New Cathedral) and turn to the right where is the CHURCH OF SAN NICCOLO' DEL SASSO, a 17th. cent. building now belonging to the schools called « Scuole Professionali Leopoldine », but once a conservatorium founded in the 13th. century by a Sienese gentlewoman called Monna Agnese. The church contains paintings by Rutilio Manetti and Francesco Vanni. A little further on are the remains of the old CHURCH OF SAN DESIDERIO; notice the sculptures on the 11th. cent. architrave.

Now the visitor should descend the stairway on the side of the Cathedral, built in 1451 by Giovanni Sabatelli. At the bottom of the flight of steps is Piazza San Giovanni with the splendid marble facade of

THE BAPTISTERY
(Battistero)

which occupies the lower back part of the Cathedral and is almost its absidal front. It occupies the basement of the prolungation of the head of the Cross of the Cathedral so it is in the place where generally the crypt is. The FACADE (fig. 29) was started in 1317 and continued in 1382 in pure Gothic style very likely to Jacopo di Mino del Pellicciaio's designs. The upper part was left unfinished and has lately been completed. It has three huge portals separated from one another by butresses; the middle portal is surmounted with a gable. Two other butresses are placed at the extremities of the facade. The central part of the facade bears a row of little pointed arches; the upper part has three blind ogival windows, the two side ones being deeper and surmounted with sharper pointed arches than the central one. In the lozenges on the lower part of the facade are

Fig. 30 - The Baptistery - *The Baptismal Font.*

human and zoomorphic heads and decorative motives. On the floor in front of the portals are graffiti, now ruined; they are *Birth and Confirmation*, by Bartolomeo di Mariano in 1450 and *Baptism*, by Antonio Federighi in 1451. The colour of the whole building is enlivened with touches of pink and red.

INTERIOR. Is probably the work of Camaino di Crescentino and Tino di Camaino. It is rectangular, the nave separated from the aisles by two pillars. The middle arch is rounded whilst the others are pointed. The vaults are cruciform, with deep ribs and the apse is poliygonal. The whole upper part is covered with frescoes ranged as follows: on the vaults looking towards the facade, *Apostles* by Vecchietta; beneath the arches *Prophets and Sibyls* (Vecchietta). On the other vaults: *the Articles of the Creed*, of the school of Vecchietta in 1450; in the right lunette *Jesus in the House of the Pharisee*, by Pietro di Francesco degli Orioli in 1489; in the apse, the *Life of Jesus*, the upper part is the work of Michele di Matteo from Bologna, the lower is of the school of Vecchietta; in the left lunette the *Miracles of St. Anthony*, by Benvenuto di Giovanni in 1453. In the niche in the left wall is a wooden statue of *John the Baptist*, of the school of Jacopo della Quercia.

In the middle of the Baptistery on a basement of steps stands the marble BAPTISMAL FONT (fig. 30), the well known masterpiece very likely drawn by Jacopo della Quercia (1416-1434). The architectural part of the work was carried out by Pietro del Minella, Bastiano del Corso and Nanni da Lucca in 1428-30; it still shows the graceful elegance of the Gothic style but the composition already enjoys the sobriety and equilibrium of the Renaissance. The Font is hexagonal and upholds an hexagonal ciborium surmounted by a little column with a capital and a pillar on which stands the statue of the *Baptist*, of the school of Jacopo della Quercia. The whole sculptural part of the work is exquisite and is due to the best artists so that the Font ranks among the greatest masterpieces of the Italian sculpture of the early Quattrocento.

The font. Starting from the panel in front of the altar: six gilt bronze bas-reliefs separated from one another by little statues are ranged as follows: 1) *Zaccaria expelled from the Temple*, by Jacopo della Quercia (the expression is severe and powerful); *Justice*, by Giovanni di Turino (1427); 2) *the Birth of St. John the Baptist*, by Turino di

Sano (1427); *Charity*, by Giovanni di Turino (1424); 3) *the Baptist Preaching*, id. (1427); *Prudence*, id.; 4) *the Baptism of Christ*, by Lorenzo Ghiberti in 1427 (this panel is delicate and expressive); *Faith*, by Donatello; 5) *the Capture of the Baptist*, by Ghiberti; *Hope*, by Donatello in 1428 (here the psychological penetration is deep); 6) *the Banquet of Herod*, id. (1427) which is the best piece of all the Font on account of its dramatic power, creative impulse and daring architecture; *Fortitude*, by Goro di Neroccio (1428).

The ciborium bears four small bronze angels on the fronts of the four panels, three of which are the work of Donatello, and one of Giovanni di Turino. Five figures of *Prophets* by Jacopo della Quercia are in the niches. On the door is the *Madonna and Child*, by Giovanni di Turino.

On the right hand corner of the Piazza is the PALAZZO DEL MAGNIFICO built for Pandolfo Petrucci the Lord of Siena, called the « Magnifico » (see page 15). It was built by Domenico di Bartolomeo from Piacenza in 1508 probably to G. Cozzarelli's designs. The bells and bronze brackets on the walls are also the work of Cozzarelli and are most admirably wrought; two of them are now just inside the entrance of the Town Hall (see page 43). When the palace was first built, the walls were decorated with frescoes by the best Italian artists such as Signorelli, Pinturicchio, Genga, but later on they were detached.

Walking along Via dei Pellegrini and then through the Costarella dei Barbieri, the visitor reaches once more Piazza del Campo.

———————

Itinerary III

FROM PIAZZA DEL CAMPO TO SANTA MARIA DEL CARMINE

(the Picture Gallery - Sant'Agostino - Santa Maria del Carmine).

From Piazza del Campo the visitor reaches Via di Città through the Chiasso del Bargello from where a most characteristic view of the Torre del Mangia can be admired. Walking along Via di Città one very soon reaches Piazza Postierla (Itinerary II) Turning left is Via di San Pietro with PALAZZO BUONSIGNORI (no. 29). This building, restored in 1848 by Giulio Rossi, is one of the finest Sienese Gothic architectures dating back to the fourteenth century. It is made of brick on a stone basement with blind arches on the lower part of the building; the first and second storeys have triple windows and are separated from one another by a cornice with little arches. Marble embrasures with sculptured busts are on the battlements. At present it is the seat of the Picture Gallery.

THE PICTURE GALLERY
(Pinacoteca)

At first it was the Gallery of the Provincial Institute of Fine Arts and only contained a small collection of old Sienese paintings belonging to Abbot Giuseppe Ciaccheri (18th. century) to which some other paintings of various origin were gradually added. In 1932 it became the State Picture Gallery and was ranged as the visitor actually sees it. It is a most complete and satisfactory compendium of Sienese painting from the very earliest times through its evolution. The rooms are ranged in chronological order starting from the second floor where the most representative works of the Sienese school are treasured, down to the first floor. Each picture bears a label with information; the catalogue of all the works in the Picture Gallery is on sale in the entrance. Here is a brief description of the most important works with their respective numbers.

THE ENTRANCE HALL AND THE COURT-YARD.

Here are some sculptures belonging to the Roman period (*Victory* : a sarcophagus with bas-reliefs) and to the late Middle Ages (three bas-reliefs with *Stories from the life of Blessed Gioacchino Piccolomini*, of the Sienese school of the 14th. century; other three bas-reliefs representing the *Annunciation, Noli me Tangere and Jesus on the way to Emmaus*, of the Sienese school of the trecento; six bas-reliefs in Pietra Serena representing the *Four Evangelists, St. Paul and Moses,* probably the work of Giovanni di Turino, and other minor works). On the left side of the courtyard is a very fine marble portal of the 17th. century which belonged to the Monastery of Monte Oliveto Minore outside Porta Tufi; it leads to the SALA DEL CENACOLO (the Hall of the Last Supper) where there is Bernardino Poccetti's fresco illustrating the subject, once the property of the Certosa di Pontignano. Some walnut pillars carved by Antonio Barili and a few statues of the 14th. century are also worthy of attention. This room is occasionally used for temporary exhibitions of ancient and modern art. On the right side of the courtyard are two rooms containing a most interesting collection of drawings of the Sienese school, some of the cartoons made by Domenico Beccafumi for the engravings on the floor of the Cathedral and the sketch for the bronze ciborium made by Vecchietta for the Church of Santa Maria della Scala, now on the high altar of the Cathedral.

THE SECOND FLOOR.

ROOMS 1-2. THE FIRST SIENESE PAINTINGS - GUIDO DA SIENA AND PAINTERS PRIOR TO DUCCIO.

Room 1. - No. 597, belonging to the Sienese school of the duecento, (the early years of the century) *the Crucifixion and six stories of the Passion of Christ;* this is one of the oldest masterpieces of Sienese painting. No. 1, Sienese School : *Christ in the act of Benediction and the Symbols of the Four Evangelists* with six stories three of which very likely about the *Raising of the Cross* and three about the *life of St. Helen.* This is the first dated

work of the Sienese school (1215). No. 8, Guido da Siena's
school (about the year 1280), *the Resurrection of Lazarus,
the Entrance into Jerusalem and the Transfiguration* : these
are the best works produced by the painters prior to
Duccio. Mark the delightful decoration in the central panel.
Next come works by some late pupil of Guido da Siena's
belonging to the Sienese school of the late thirteenth century, and a few Byzantine Sienese works (about 1290).

Room 2. - No. 14, a Sienese-Byzantine altar screen belonging more or less to the year 1270 with *St. John the Baptist
seated on a throne and, on the sides, twelve stories from
the life.* In the middle is the *Saint in the act of
benediction after the Greek way;* these panels show both
Gothic and Byzantine influences but the colours are bright
and the perspective daring (mark the scene of *Salomé's
Dance* and that of the *Birth of the Baptist*). No. 15, this work
is ascribed to Guido da Siena : an altar screen with
St. Peter seated on a throne and on the sides six stories
of his life, *the Annunciation* and *the Nativity of Jesus*

Fig. 31 - Picture Gallery - 34,
Ugolino di Nerio: *The Crucifixion.*

Fig. 32 - Picture Gallery - 20,
Duccio: *The Madonna of the
Franciscans.*

Fig. 33 - Picture Gallery - 65, Ambrogio Lorenzetti: *Enthroned Madonna with six Angels and six Saints.*

Christ: here the freshness of the colours is remarkable, though not quite free from Byzantine influences. Next come some interesting works by Margaritone di Arezzo, by some pupils of Guido da Siena's and by an anonymous Sienese painter of the later half of the 13th. century.

ROOMS 3-4. DUCCIO DI BUONINSEGNA AND HIS SCHOOL.

Room 3. - No. 23, is a work ascribed to Duccio di Buoninsegna (1260-1319); it is a fragment of a many-panelled picture representing *St. Mary Magdalene,* most precious for the rare beauty of the style and expression (remark the beautiful head of the Madonna). No. 47, the back of an altar piece by Duccio di Buoninsegna with the *Holy Virgin and Child, St. John the Baptist and St. Mary Magdalene, St. John the Evangelist and St. Agnes;* above them are *Prophets and Patriarchs, four Angels and the Redeemer in the act of Benediction;* though solemn, the Madonna has an expression of humility whilst the lateral figures, probably the work of some pupil, seem full of energy (especially St. John the Baptist); some of the Prophets are remarkable for the power of their expression. No. 28 is a many panelled painting by Duccio di Buoninsegna representing the *Virgin and the Holy Child with St. Paul, St. Agostine, St. Peter and St. Domininic;* in the gables, the *Redeemer in the act of Benediction and four Angels;* the attitudes of these figures are remarkably natural and their expression most powerful (especially St. Agostine's and St. Peter's). Besides, there are : by Ugolino di Nerio (...1317-1327...) a most beautiful *Crucifixion* marked no. 34 (see fig. 31) and works by Niccolò di Segna (...1381-1345...), by a disciple of Segna di Bonaventura and other Sienese painters of the early years of the 14th. century. The door in front of the entrance leads to

Room 4. - No. 35, is a triptych with little doors belonging to Duccio school painted with the figures of *Majesty, Saints and Scenes from the New Testament;* an exquisite work of art. No. 593, by Maestro di Badia a Isola (the end of the 13th. century), is a restored *Madonna and Child;* this painting is original only in some of its parts (see the Child's little foot). No. 20 is a delightful work by Duccio di Buoninsegna, *the Madonna and Holy Child with three adoring Franciscans* (the style is Gothic-Byzantine, see fig. 32) which is most eloquent on account of the expressive power of the « line » remark the border of the Virgin's cloak, the wings of the Angels and the profiles of the kneeling friars and of the « decoration » (remark the pannelled background). Besides, there are works by Segna di Bonaventura and Ugolino di Nerio.

Room 5. (Corridor).

No. 58, by one of Naddo Ceccarelli's followers. No. 50 is a *Polyptych* by Pietro Lorenzetti dating back to 1335 or 1340.

Room 6. THE LORENZETTI BROTHERS AND THE SIENESE PAINTERS OF THE 14TH. CENTURY.

No. 116, the *Nativity of Mary, St. Jacob, St. Catherine of Alexandria, St. Bartholomew and St. Elizabeth of Hungury*, is the masterpiece of Paolo di Giovanni Fei (...1369-1411). The scene of the Nativity echoes the art of Pietro Lorenzetti (see the Museum of the Cathedral, page 89) with a profusion of well related details. No. 77, by Ambrogio Lorenzetti (...1318-1348) *the Madonna and Holy Child with St. Mary Magdalene and St. Dorothy* (a part of a panelled picture; see fig. 34); No. 77a by the same artist, *the Deposition* which was probably meant for the basis of no. 77.

Fig. 34 – Picture Gallery – 77, Ambrogio Lorenzetti: *The Madonna with St. Dorothy and St. Mary Magdalene*.

Fig. 35 - Picture Gallery - 88, Ambrogio Lorenzetti: *The
Annunciation.*

The two Saints are paying homages to the Virgin. St. Dorothy, the sweeter of the two figures is carrying corn-
flowers and other bright coloured flowers, St. Magdalene
is offering sweet scented ointments. The scene of the deposition, instead, is dramatic and becomes even tragic with
the group around Christ. No. 65, by Ambrogio Lorenzetti,
*Enthroned Madonna with the Holy Child surrounded by
six Angels and six Saints* (fig. 33). This is an unmistakable
masterpiece. The harmonic lines of the figures stand out
in relief on the pleasant chromatic ground where gold
used as a colour prevails; the story seems to start from
the vase of flowers in the middle of the composition, mov-
ing upwards, phrase after phrase, to the top of the lobe.

No. 605, by Ambrogio Lorenzetti, *the Madonna and Holy
Child*. This scene is full of human feeling; the little Child
has one arm lovingly round his Mother's neck and is timidly
clasping her veil. No. 70 and 71, by Ambrogio Lorenzetti,
are *two views of seaside towns* which are the first specimen
of landscape painting which have reached us. Very likely
they were meant as the decoration of a coffer; however their
importance is great both as to their intrinsic value and to

Fig. 36 - Picture Gallery - Pietro Lorenzetti: *The Madonna of the
Carmine* (no number).

what originated from them in later centuries. They are most fanciful works with a peculiar charm arising from the repetition of certain tones of greenish-blue with a few wise touches of red. No. 88, *the Annunciation*, by Ambrogio Lorenzetti, dated 1344 (fig. 35). This work has often been discussed and compared with the famous *Annunciation* painted by Simone Martini, now in the Uffizi Picture Gallery in Florence. Ambrogio makes us feel the presence of Divinity through the exhaltation of the plastic perspective and expressive values as if all the resources of human spirituality were exaggerated (God is at the summit of spirituality of which Man is but an active part : immanentism and pantheism) ; with Simone Martini, instead, the beauty of his linearism reaches the form of a dream and tries to escape from the world be it spiritual or corporeal ; it is pure mysticism (the essence of God is unknown to the human spirit even though postulated : dualism, transcendentalism). Now comes a work without a number, by Pietro Lorenzetti (1280-1348 ?) representing the so called *Madonna del Carmine* with *the Holy Child and Saints* (fig. 36) which comes from the Confraternita di Sant'Ansano a Dofana. No. 83-84 is a central panel with four smaller ones, by Pietro Lorenzetti representing *Pope Honorius* giving a new habit to the Friars of Carmine ; the same *Pope sanctions the Order of the Carmelites ; the Carmelite Friars at the Font ; Sobac's dream*. All these paintings once belonged to one same altar in the Church of the Carmelites in Siena (la Chiesa del Carmine). Remarkable are the smaller scenes told with very few essential touches of pure gem-like colours, precise in space and perspective (especially Sobac's dream and the Carmelite Friars at the Font).

The works numbered 578, 579, 64, 62 are by Pietro Lorenzetti ; the fine many-panelled painting number 300 is the work of Paolo di Giovanni Fei ; « *Maestà* » no. 80 is by Jacopo di Mino del Pelliociaio (1330-1410) and no. 61 is Maestro di San Pietro a Ovile's *Assunta,* both worthy of notice. Then come a few works of the school of Ambrogio Lorenzetti and of Maestro di San Lucchese.

On the right hand side looking towards the entrance are

ROOMS 7-8. - LIPPO MEMMI AND MINOR PAINTERS OF THE 14TH CENTURY

Room 7. - No. 104, *the Adoration of the Magi,* by Bartolo di Fredi (1330-1410). It is one of the author's masterpieces remarkable for the animation of the details and the bright enamel-like decoration (fig. 46). No. 162, *the Stigmata of St. Francis,* ascribed to Taddeo di Bartolo (1363-1422), is a charming painting. There are also some good paintings by

Bartolo di Fredi. Taddeo di Bartolo and Luca di Tommé (...1356-1389). Worthy of special attention is the panelled painting no. 586 representing the figure of *Majesty among Saints* by a disciple of Luca di Tommé's. By Niccolò di Ser Sozzo Tegliacci (..1334-1363) is another *Majesty with Angels and Saints* - number 51; next come works by Paolo di Giovanni Fei, Martino di Bartolomeo and Bartolomeo Bulgarini.

Room 8. - No. 595, *the Madonna and the Holy Child,* by Lippo Memmi (...1317-1356...); it is one of the best works produced by this worthly disciple of Simone Martini's; No. 108, *St. Catherine's Mystic Wedding,* by Maestro della Madonna di Palazzo Venezia is a very accurate work. Besides, there are works by Niccolò di Buonaccorso, by a disciple of Lippo Memmi (the so called Maestro di S. Paolo), by a late imitator of Lippo Memmi, by Benedetto di Bindo and Naddo Ceccarelli.

Now the visitor must go back through room 7 and room 6 to reach

ROOM 9. PAINTERS OF THE 14TH. CENTURY (1320-1330).

Here are works by Maestro di Città di Castello, by Maestro di Chianciano, by one of Duccio di Buoninsegna's disciples, by an artist of the school of Niccolò di Segna and by an artist known as « Maestro della Maestà di Londra » (the Master of the figure of Majesty in London). No. 92, *the Allegory of Sin and Redemption,* by Pietro Lorenzetti though this authorship is still discussed. It is a work of high mastery, with a strong dramatic power which transfigures the allegory and turns it into a definite scene (as often happens with Ambrogio Lorenzetti's frescoes in the Palazzo Comunale) : the landscape echoes the everlasting human tragedy rather than appearing as a backround.

By a little door next to this room the visitor now reaches the staircase called the SCALA DELLA PIA (see page 123). It is a winding staircase with a quaint perspective.

ROOM 10. (The Corridor and Loggia). - SIENESE AND FLORENTINE PAINTERS.
(*First corridor*) - Works by Spinello Aretino (1352?-1410), by Niccolò di Pietro Gerini and by Andrea di Bartolo (...1389-1428).

ROOM 11. (Ante-Chapel and Chapel).

Works by Paolo di Giovanni Fei (remarkable is no. 146 representing *the Madonna seated on a throne between Saints*) and by an anonymous Sienese painter of the 14th.

— 110 —

Fig. 37 - Picture Gallery - 211, Giovanni di Paolo: *The Presentation of Jesus in the Temple.*

century. In the 18th. century Chapel there is a spoilt polychrome terracotta representing *Magdalene* ascribed to Giacomo Cozzarelli (1453-1515).

ROOM 12. TADDEO DI BARTOLO AND THE LAST PAINTERS OF THE
14TH. CENTURY.

No. 131 is a many-panelled picture representing the *Annunciation, Saints and Archangel Gabriel,* by Taddeo di
Bartolo; it is an imposing and solemn work not entirely
free from Simone Martini's influence (see the chromatic
tones of the clothes and wings of the Angel). No. 128 is a
triptych representing the *Madonna seated upon a throne
with the Holy Babe, Saints,* the *Crucifixion and the Annunciation,* by the same author. It is one of the master's most
refined works where some of the faces are quite characteristic. No. 127 represents the *Adoration of the Magi,* by
Taddeo di Bartolo, a most delicate work. No. 55, the *Crucifix,* one of Taddeo di Bartolo's most precious works on
account of the accuracy of the drawing and of the masterly
skill in portraying the face of Christ. A few minor works
by Taddeo di Bartolo come next and then other works by
Andrea di Bartolo, Martino di Bartolommeo (...1389-1434...),
Gualtieri di Giovanni and by Maestro della Vita di Maria
(the Master of the life of Mary).

Going back into the CORRIDOR the visitor now sees the
last part of it with the works produced by Bernardo Daddi
(...1312-1348...) and by a Master of his school, by Antonio
Veneziano (...1369-1388...), Mariotto di Nardo (...1394-1424...),
Giovanni del Biondo (...1356-1392...) and Rossello di Jacopo
Franchi (...1376?-1456?). Most remarkable is picture no. 157,
by Lorenzo Monaco (1370?-1422?), representing the *Madonna
with the Holy Babe, Saints and the Annunciation.*

Now go back to the bottom of the corridor and turn to
the left into

ROOMS 13-14. GIOVANNI DI PAOLO AND SASSETTA.

Room 13. - No. 324 and 186, 187, 188, 189 are by Giovanni
di Paolo (1399-1482); this many-panelled picture represents
the *Madonna dell'Assunta among Angel-musicians, at her
sides are four Saints, on the altar steps « Pietà » and Saints
and four other Saints on the pillars.* It is a sumptuous representation of the scene which brings something new and
grandiose to the Master's usual decorative skill (remarkable is the group of the Angels playing upon their instruments; they are worthy of Botticelli). No. 200, the *Crucifixion, the Madonna, Mary Magdalene and St. John,* by
Giovanni di Paolo. These figures are represented in utmost
sorrow: the group is dominated by the figure of St. John.

LORENZO DI PIETRO detto IL VECCHIETTA
(Siena, 1412-1480)

Il Beato Pier Pettinaio (Pinacoteca)
Le Bienheureux Pier Pettinaio (Pinacothèque)
Blessed Pier Pettinaio (Art Gallery)
Der sel. Pier Pettinaio (Pinakothek)

V.

No. 212, *Christ Suffering and Christ Trimphant,* by Giovanni di Paolo. The mastery of the drawing and chiaroscuro is remarkable, especially in the face of Christ Suffering. No. 174, 175 and 176 represent the *Presentation of Mary in the Temple, the Crucifixion* and *the Flight to Egypt,* by Giovanni di Paolo; the landscape of this last work shows the Master's skill and lyrical fantasy at its best. No. 198, *Scenes from the Life of the Madonna and of Saints,* by Giovanni di Paolo; this painting has a rare value on account of the few fundamental colours used (remark the happy blue tones). Next come some of Giovanni di Paolo's minor works and a panel by Sano di Pietro (1406-1481).

Room 14. - No. 325, *the Madonna seated on a Throne with the Holy Child,* by Stefano di Giovanni nicknamed Sassetta (1392-1450). No. 206, *the Madonna and Holy Babe,* by Giovanni di Paolo; the bushes in full bloom, the fine castles the spiral form of the sloping hills create an enchanting atmosphere around the figure of the Madonna. No. 211, *the Presentation in the Temple,* by Giovanni di Paolo (fig. 37). The perspective of the temple is so complex as to create an optical illusion; this picture was inspired by the same scene painted by Ambrogio Lorenzetti, actually in the Uffizi Picture Gallery in Florence; however, the colours are pleasing. The picture no. 654 represents the same scene but is not so worthy of appreciation. No. 172, *the Last Judgement, Paradise and Hell,* by Giovanni di Paolo (1460-65); here the Master reveals, one might say, the other side of his personality which aims at « reality » when dealing with figures feelings and things; the scenes are pervaded with pleasant simplicity. The tragedy in many scenes is mitigated, and the bounding joy reduced to the pleasant exchange of affectionate courtesies. No. 177, *the Madonna and the Holy Babe among four Angels with St. Catherine of Alexandria and St. John the Baptist* at her sides by the « Maestro dell'Osservanza »; the composition of this picture is most sweet. Delightful, above all, are the faces of the Angels holding up the Madonna's veil and the face of St. Catherine. Besides these works there are other minor works by Giovanni di Paolo and Sassetta, and paintings by pseudo Pellegrino di Mariano and Pietro di Giovanni di Ambrogio (1410-1449).

ROOMS 15-16-17. MATTEO DI GIOVANNI, NEROCCIO DI BARTOLOMMEO LANDI, FRANCESCO DI GIORGIO MARTINI AND PAINTERS OF THE LATE YEARS OF THE 15TH CENTURY.

Room 15. - No. 283, *the Madonna and Child,* by Matteo di Giovanni (1430 ?-1495); the landscape is very sweet. No. 294,

Fig. 38 - Picture Gallery - 437,
Francesco di Giorgio Martini:
The Nativity.

Fig. 39 - Picture Gallery - 286,
Matteo di Giov.: *The Madonna and Holy Child.*

the Madonna and Child, by Neroccio di Bartolommeo Landi
(1447-1500). This picture is a masterpiece; it is fresh,
harmonic and lively and the colours are most fluent (the
face of the Virgin is masterly). No. 286, *the Madonna and
Child* (fig. 39) by Matteo di Giovanni. Most interesting is
the delicate sweet human face of the Madonna with a faint
smile lingering on her lips, and also the chubby little Child,
the happy faces of the angels and the graceful flowers (dated
1470). No. 281, *the Madonna with the Holy Child and two
Saints,* by Neroccio di Bartolommeo Landi (fig. 40). The
chromatic technique of this painting is almost modern; the
whole tonality is ash pink. The Virgin has a mysterious
dreamy and absent expression and is holding the Child
lightly on her lap. No. 277, *the Annunciation* by Francesco
di Giorgio Martini (1439-1502). The chromatic tones of this
picture are sometimes rather hard but the scene is elegant
and happily expressed. No. 437, *the Nativity,* a signed
masterpiece by Francesco di Giorgio Martini (fig. 38). A soft
spring morning light illuminates the scene and all the
figures are joyous as the event requires. No. 293, *the Madonna and Child with two Saints,* by Francesco di Giorgio

Fig. 40 - Picture Gallery - 281, Neroccio di Bartolommeo
Landi: *The Madonna and Holy Child with two Saints.*

Martini; here, the iconography is quite peculiar and the drawing most accurate. Then come other less important works by Matteo di Giovanni, Neroccio di Bartolommeo Landi, Francesco di Giorgio Martini, Guidoccio Cozzarelli (...1450-1516) the master who produced the fine picture of *St. Sebastian,* number 296. No. 363 is the *Madonna and Child,* by Bernardino Fungai (1460-1516), remarkable for the beauty of the colours.

ROOM 16. - Contains works by Neroccio di Bartolommeo Landi and Pietro di Domenico (1457-1503?). Worthy of attention is no. 279 representing the *Adoring Shepherds* (fig. 42) and no. 390 representing the *Nativity of Christ* where the landscape is almost like a miniature. Number 445, by Guidoccio Cozzarelli, represents *St. Catherine in the act of receiving the Heart of Jesus.* Next come works by Lorenzo di Pietro nicknamed Vecchietta, Francesco di Giorgio Martini, Bernardino Fungai, by a follower of Matteo di Giovanni's (remarkable is no. 446, the *Madonna and Holy Child*), by Girolamo di Benvenuto (1470-1524) and by one of Benvenuto di Giovanni's disciples.

ROOM 17. - No. 431, *the Madonna and Holy Child among Saints,* by Bernardino Fungai. This picture bears the date 1512 and is one of the Master's best works. No. 204 is a reliquary painted on both sides by Vecchietta (1412-1480) with *Figures of Saints* (outside) and *Scenes from the Sacred History* (inside) which are the most interesting. No. 440 *is the Coronation of the Virgin among Angels and Saints,* by Francesco di Giorgio Martini. The scene is animated, very good in the lower right part, but the blending of the colours is rather harsh though with rich effects. Other works by Francesco di Giorgio Martini follow, and by Vecchietta, Girolamo di Benvenuto, Giacomo Pacchiarotti, Andrea di Niccolò (1450?-1529) and Sano di Pietro.

ROOMS 18-19-20. SANO DI PIETRO.

These three rooms are devoted to the abundant production of Sano di Pietro (1406-1481) and enable the visitor to discover the secret of his style which still shows Gothic reminiscences; his pecliar stroke excells in bright effects and in the composition of the scenes. Most worthy of attention is

ROOM 18. - No. 241, *the Madonna appears to Calistus III;* this is a masterpiece of perspective synthesis, signed and dated 1456 (fig. 41). No. 246 is a many-pannelled picture representing the *Madonna seated upon a throne with the Holy Child, Angels and Saints;* the colours are delightful:

ROOM 19. - Here are treasured some very large many-

Fig. 41 - Picture Gallery - 241,
Sano di Pietro: *The Madonna
appears to Pope Calistus III.*

Fig. 42 - Picture Gallery - 279,
Pietro di Domenico: *The Adoring Shepherds.*

panelled pictures provided with foot-boards and steps, numbered 269, 255, 226, 233 and 259; the best of them are no. 233 and no. 259. Number 227 represents the *Assumption of the Madonna among Angels and Saints;* it is one of the Master's best compositions though rather damaged.

Room 20. - No. 237, a triptych representing the *Madonna and Holy Child, Angels and Saints* and *the Annunciation;* this work is archaic but the decorative taste is good and the expression also. No. 265, *St. Jerome Penitent;* a scene full of emotion on an intensely evocative background.

Now the visitor must descend to

THE FIRST FLOOR

and turn to the right, on the steps, where are

ROOMS 21-22-23. SIENESE AND UMBRIAN MASTERS AND OTHER PAINTERS OF THE 15TH. AND 16TH. CENTURIES.

Room 21. - No. 581, *Noli me Tangere,* by Benvenuto di Giovanni (1436-1518); no. 388, the *Madonna and Child,* by Giacomo Pacchiarotti (1474-1539); no. 366, *the Figures of Five*

Saints, by Giacomo Pacchiarotti; no. 309, *the Annunciation,* by Girolamo da Cremona (...1467-1481); this is an exceptional work the colours of which are as bright as gems and the figure of the announcing Angel delightful. No. 298, the *Madonna and Holy Child with Saints,* (1500), by Andrea di Niccolò (1450?-1529). Now turn to the left and enter

Room 22. (Recent acquisitions and restored pictures).

In this room are gathered pictures from other collections waiting to be placed elsewhere, and pictures which have been restored in the Picture Gallery Laboratories. Notice Simone Martini's *Madonna and Child,* painted some time between 1320 and 1325. It was discovered in 1957 beneath a worthless 16th. cent. work and is one of this Master's most remarkable productions.

Room 23 - No. 209, *The Adoration of Infant Jesus, and Saints* by Pier Francesco Fiorentino; it is a typical work of this disciple of Matteo Balducci's. No. 346, *an adoring Angel* by Matteo Balducci. No. 383 is the *Assumption of the Virgin* by Cosimo Rosselli. The picture with no number represents the *Madonna and Holy Child with Saints,* painted by Neri di Bicci (1482).

Room 24. - No. 387, the *Madonna with the Holy Child and St. John* ascribed to Pinturicchio (1454-1518) is a very good work but not one of the best. No. 406, an altar piece with the scene of the *Deposition of Christ in the Temple* and, on the side, the *Stigmata of St. Francis and of St. Catherine,* by Matteo Balducci (...1509-1555). This painting bears evidence of the sweet Umbrian manner, especially the landscape. No. 422, the *Ascension of Jesus,* is one of Giacomo Pacchiarotti's best compositions. No. 334, *Aeneas fleeing from Troy,* by Girolamo Genga (1476-1551); the drawing is most efficacious and full of movement. No. 495 is the *Holy Family,* a very sweet and natural group by Pinturicchio. Besides, there are a few other works by Giacomo Pacchiarotti, Matteo Balducci, Bernardino Fungai, Girolamo Genga, a disciple of Piero della Francesca and Eusebio da San Giorgio.

Room 25. (The Loggia).

No. 68 is the *Allegory* of the Royal Palace of Siena (about the year 1650) by Francesco Maffei. No. 633 is *the Deposition,* an 18th century work by Giuseppe Bazzani.

Room 26. SIENESE PAINTERS OF THE 17TH CENTURY AND OTHER PAINTERS.

No. 625, the *Marthyrdom of Sant'Ansano,* a work by Ru-

Fig. 43 - Picture Gallery - 352, Sodoma: *Christ bound to the column.*

tilio Manetti (1571-1639) where the distribution of shade and light is already after the style of Caravaggio. No. 626, *Sant'Eligio*, Rutilio Manetti's masterpiece. No. 630, *St. Anne teaching the Madonna to read,* by Domenico Manetti (1609-1663). No. 477, the *Game of Morra,* by Antiveduto della Grammatica (...1570-1626); this work was once ascribed to Caravaggio whose stroke and peculiar way of dealing with light is here well imitated. The other paintings are by Domenico Manetti, Sismondio Salimbeni, Alessandro Casolani and Guido Canlassi.

ROOM 27. (A Turret). MINOR 17TH CENTURY PAINTERS.

Here are gathered works by Rutilio Manetti, by a Genovese master of the 17 century, by Astolfo Petrazzi and by an anonymuos Tuscan painter of the 17th century.

ROOM 28. FLORENTINE PAINTERS OF THE 16TH CENTURY.

There are paintings by G. Antonio Lappoli, Giorgio Vasari, Salviati, by painters of the Florentine school of the 16th. century, by Mariotto Albertinelli and by one of Sodoma's disciples.

ROOM 29 - This little room contains works by Andrea Piccinelli nicknamed Brescianino who worked in Siena from 1507 to 1525.

ROOM 30. SIENESE PAINTERS OF THE 16TH CENTURY.

No. 410, *the Annunciation and Visitation,* by Girolamo del Pacchia (1477-1535). No. 444 and no. 447, *the Coronation of the Virgin among Saints* and *Scenes from the Sacred History, Angels and Saints,* by Bartolommeo Neroni nicknamed Riccio (1520-1573?). No. 402 and no. 442, a *Column with Figures of Saints,* by Bartolommeo Neroni nicknamed Riccio. Besides some other of Pacchia's works, in this room there are works by some disciple of Sodoma's, by a follower of the school of Beccafumi, by Michelangelo Anselmi and Girolamo Siciolante da Sermoneta.

ROOMS 31-32-33-34. SODOMA, BECCAFUMI AND OTHER ARTISTS OF THE 16TH. CENTURY.

Room 31. - No. 384, a triptych representing the *Trinity and four Saints,* by Domenico Beccafumi (1486-1551); though a youthful work, it anticipates the Master's late luminism. No. 438, *the Madonna with the Holy Child and Saints,* by Domenico Beccafumi. No. 357, *St. Catherine of Siena,* by Giovanni Antonio Bazzi called Sodoma (1477-1549). No. 448, *the Holy Family with St. Catherine of Siena,* by Girolamo del Pacchia. No. 512, *the Nativity,* a very precious work of Sodoma's belonging to the period called pre-Leonard; this

Fig. 44 - Picture Gallery - 420, Beccafumi: *St. Catherine of Siena receives the Stigmata.*

characteristic way of painting is plainly visible in the very few touches of chiaroscuro. No. 433, *the Madonna with the Holy Child and Saints,* by Girolamo Genga; the freshness of the colours is remarkable. No. 409, *the Madonna with the Holy Child and Saints,* by A. Brescianino. Besides these works there are some by Girolamo del Pacchia, by Pomarancio, Brescianino and Giomo del Sodoma.

Room 32. - No. 352, *Christ bound to the Column* (fig. 43); this picture is considered to be Sodoma's masterpiece (delightful is the fluidity of the colours and of the forms, the beauty of the chiaroscuro and, above all, the subdued imploring expression in the exhausted eyes of Christ). No. 610, *the Crucifixion,* by Sodoma; the disposition of the figures grouped round the foot of the cross shows Piedmontese reminiscences but the landscape is typically Sodoma's. No. 369 the *Deposition from the Cross,* by Girolamo di Benvenuto (1470-1524).

Room 33. - N. 326, 327, 360 and 361, by Sodoma, *Head of a coffin* with - respectively - *Two brethren adoring the Cross, Pity, Madonna with holy child;* all these are among the most natural and inspired works of the Master who painted them about 1527; No. 413, *the Deposition from the Cross* is one of Sodoma's best youthful works; though this composition is rather complex the master has attained great beauty of forms and expression. Painted on the foot-board are *Five Stories from the Life of Christ,* by some artist of the school of Sodoma.

Room 34. - No. 420, *St. Catherine receives the Stigmata* by Beccafumi (fig. 44), the composition of this scene is quite original, the perspective daring, the landscape evanescent but precise. No. 405, *the Nativity of the Madonna,* is a very happy specimen of Beccafumi's skill in distributing chiaroscuro; the light is so vivid as to become almost dazzling. No. 344, *the Baptism of Christ,* by Beccafumi. No. 354, *Judith,* by Sodoma. No. 307, *the Self Portrait* of Francesco Vanni (1563-1610).

ROOM 35. GERMAN AND FLEMISH MASTERS.

No. 501, *St. Jerome,* by Albrecht Dürer (1471-1528) a work of great value. No. 537, *Lucretia,* by an artist of the school of Luca Cranach (1472-1553). No. 545, *the Holy Family,* either by Theodor Von Thulden (1606-1676) or by P. P. Rubens (1577-1640). A few other paintings by Flemish and German artist are also to be seen.

ROOM 36. ITALIAN ARTISTS of the 17th. century.

No. 521, *St. Francis,* by Bernardo Strozzi (1581-1644). No. 513, *the Rape of Europe,* by Padovanino (1588-1648). No. 484, a *Portrait,* by G.B. Moroni (1520?-1578). No. 522, *the Portrait of a Young Man,* by Girolamo Mazzola Bedoli (1500?-1569), the colour is delightful and the psychologic penetration of the subject very deep. Besides these works there are some by Bernardino Poccetti (1548-1612), Paolo Farinati (1524-1606), Federico Zuccari (1524?-1609), Francesco Montemezzano (1540?-1602?) and Scarsellino (1551-1620).

ROOM 37. VENETIAN MASTERS.

No. 456, *the Madonna and Christ* by A. Bartolommeo Montagna (1450-1523). No. 163, *the Nativity,* by Lorenzo Lotto (1480-1556); the effect of this picture is based on strong contrasting colours, very expressive and well controlled. No. 544, *the Madonna with the Holy Babe, Sant'Omobono and the donor;* this is a typical Venetian picture on account of the warm chromatic effect. It is ascribed to Paris Bordone (1500-1571). No. 544, *the Annunciation,* by Paris Bordone; the perspective of the colonnade is good and the mountains in the landscape are vibrating with light. No. 539, the *Brazen Serpent,* by Jacopo Palma Junior (il Giovane) (1544-1628). No. 467, *the Portrait of a Man,* by G. B. Moroni.

ROOM 38. BECCAFUMI AND SODOMA.

No. 427, *Jesus in Limbo,* by Domenico Beccafumi; this painting is a masterpiece of colour and light (remark Christ's mantle) and form (notice the splendid figure of the Good Thief on the left) and of composition. It is complex and new, the style perfect. No. 423, the *Fall of the Angels,* a fine study of nude figures by D. Beccafumi. No. 401, *the Agony in the Garden,* a detached fresco by Sodoma. No. 443, the *Descent of Jesus to Limbo,* a detached and spoilt fresco by Sodoma; the conception, here, is quite different to that of the same picture by Beccafumi (no. 427) though Beccafumi drew inspiration from Sodoma for the figure of his modest Eve. The colours of this painting are light and luminous, the whole composition is rich and lively as no other work by this Master.

Coming out of the Picture Gallery turn to the left; house no. 31 is supposed to be the « CASA DELLA PIA » (the House of Pia, the unhappy Sienese gentlewoman mentioned by Dante in his *Purgatory,* (vv. 133-136). It is an ancient Gothic building belonging to the noble Pannocchieschi family, with ogival double windows and slender columns. According to tradition, in this house Pia - the daughter of Buonconte Guastelloni and widow of Baldo Tolomei - was married to Nello Pannocchieschi who, later on, kept her a prisoner in a castle in Maremma called « Castello di Pietra » until she died, because he believed she was unfaithful; hence Dante's verses read: « *Siena mi fe', disfecemi Maremma* ». (Siena made me, Maremma destroyed me).

On the top of the flight of steps on the left side of the little square is the CHURCH OF S. PIETRO ALLE SCALE or in Castelvecchio. It was built in the 13th. century but was completely re-built in the 18th. The facade has a good portal with a spandrel and butresses and a brick cornice and coping. There is only one nave and a small transept resting on different styled columns. *Left wall*: on the first altar is a picture of the *Madonna dell'Assunta* by Rustichino. Over the high alter is a picture representing the *Flight to Egypt,* by Rutilio Manetti (1621); the warm, well illuminated group of the Madonna with the Holy Babe and young St. John emerge from the dark background whilst the other personages behind them can hardly be seen; dazzling are, instead, the joyful Angels hovering over them. In the nearby Parsonage are treasured the following pictures: a *Madonna* by Sano di Pietro, formerly inside the Church; *St. Lucy and Archangel Gabriel* by the same artist; *four Saints* by Ambrogio Lorenzetti (1344); *Christ in the act of Benedicting* by Giovanni di Paolo and a *Madonna* by some artis of the Lorenzetti brothers' school.

Now walk along Via S. Pietro and pass beneath the ARCH OF SANT'AGOSTINO otherwise called PORTA ALL'ARCO; (in the 15th. century it marked the limits of the town) into « Prato di Sant'Agostino ». where there is the long side wall of the

BASILICA OF ST. AUGUSTINE
(Basilica di Sant'Agostino)

which dates back to the year 1253. The apse, however, was completed in the 14th. century and later on the facade was joined to the Convent (since 1818 the seat of the school called CONVITTO NAZIONALE TOLOMEI) by a porch under which is the entrance to the Church.

THE INTERIOR is well illuminated, shaped like a Latin cross with but one nave. It was entirely re-built by Luigi Vanvitelli in 1755.

Right wall: first altar: the *Communion of St. Jerome*, by Astolfo Petrazzi (1631). Second altar, the *Crucifixion*, by Perugino (1506); remark the affectionate familiar expression on the faces of the women at the foot of the cross and the pretty landscape; both these features are quite peculiar to Perugino. Fouth altar: *Jesus falls while carrying the Cross*, by Ventura Salimbeni in 1612. Enter the right transept and ring the bell on the Sacristy door to be admitted into the *Piccolomini Chapel* where the treasures of art belonging to the Church are kept. Over the altar is the *Epiphany*, a masterpiece painted by Sodoma in 1518; the colours are beautiful and in a perfect state of preservation, the chiaroscuro soft and rich, the rocky mountains on the horizon the best the Master ever painted (some believe that Sodoma's own face is peeping between the trunks of the two larger trees). On the right wall (looking towards the altar) a triptych by Simone Martini celebrating *Blessed Agostino Novello* (1320). In the centre stands the figure of Agostino, above him are two Augustinian Saints. On either sides are two panels with the representation of some of the miracles worked by Blessed Agostino with a scene of thanksgiving in each picture. Here the linearism which has almost become Simone Martini's stylistic emblem seems less accentuated but the precision of the drawing instead is extreme, the elegance of each element and of the whole composition most worthy of praise. The scene of the *Knight's Miracle*, for instance, is most powerful, the architecture full of fancy and colour, the background, as usual, rocky. Left wall: *the Massacre of the Innocents* painted by Matteo di Giovanni in 1482; the iconography of this picture reminds one of the picture of the same subject actually in the Basilica of S. Maria dei Servi (see page 148). The face of the author is believed to be portrayed in the head appearing beneath Herod's arm. In the lunette facing the altar is a fresco of the *Madonna seated on a throne among Saints*, by Ambrogio Lorenzetti. This painting has only recently been discovered; this accounts for its being damaged though the tones of blue red and brown in the right part are stil amazingly bright. Below: a wooden statue of the *Madonna and Holy Child* formerly ascribed to Jacopo della Quercia, now to Niccolò de' Cori or, maybe, to Mattia di Nanni di Stefano nicknamed Bernacchino; it is a fifteenth century work. On the walls are some pictures painted by artists of the 17th. century.

Next to the Chapel is a little room containing the statue of Pius II, by Giovanni Duprè in 1858. Now go back to the church and enter the right transept. The second chapel on the right hand side of the high altar has a picture of *St. Cristopher* over the altar, painted by Niccolò Franchini in 1755; on the right wall is *Jesus being baptised by St. John*, by Stefano Volpi during the 17th. century. On the left wall two *Saints* by Giovanni Bruni in 1853. The floor is covered with little enamel terracotta tiles produced by Pietro e Niccolò Mazzaburroni in 1488. The wooden confessionals are worthy of attention. First Chapel on the right of the high altar: over the altar is an anonymous seventeenth century picture of the *Madonna;* on the walls two pictures by Bruni. The grandiose marble altar is a very fine work of art produced by Flaminio del Turco; the statues of the Angels are by Bartolomeo Mazzuoli. Beneath the altar is the urn containing the ashes of Blessed Agostino Novello. Left transept: right wall of the first chapel: *San Giuseppe Calasanzio and the Madonna*, by Sebastiano Conca. Second chapel: the *Temptation of Sant'Agostino Abate*, by Rutilio Manetti; remark the gloomy light in the background and the good distribution of shade and light. On the back of the transept: on the altar a painted wooden statue of *San Nicola da Tolentino*, by Giacomo Cozzarelli. Left wall of the nave: fourth altar: *St. Augustine and the Angel*, by Pietro Sorri in 1600. Third altar: the *Baptism of Constantine*, by Francesco Vanni in 1586. Second altar: the *Immaculate Conception*, by Carlo Maratta in 1671. First altar: the *Crib*, by Giovanni Francesco Romanelli (17th. century).

In a little square near « Prato di Sant'Agostino » is the little CHURCH OF SANTA MUSTIOLA. The old brick structure made to hold the bells under two little ogive arches is still to be seen and in the precincts of the old Convent are now ranged the MUSEUMS OF THE ACCADEMIA DEI FISIOCRITICI (the Academy of Physiocritics) founded in 1680 by Pirro Maria Gabbrielli. These Museums exhibit specimens of different kinds of soil, fossils, saurians, chelonids, fishes, mammals, birds, serpents, molluscs, insects, crustacea, minerals, rocks and paleolithic objects.

[From here, turning to the right through the fourteenth century gateway called PORTA TUFI (ascribed to Agnolo di Ventura) one reaches the MISERICORDIA CEMETERY lying on the spot where, till the 14th. century, stood the Monastery of the Olivetan Friars known as Monteoliveto Minore. Many Chapels in this cemetery contain fine artistic monuments; of wide fame are Tito Sarrocchi's marble groups representing the *Genius of Death* sculp-

Fig. 45 – St. Joseph's Arch.

tured in 1860; *Tobias* in 1872; *Ezechiel* in 1881 and Giovanni Duprè's group of « *Pietà* » (1875)].

Leaving Prato di Sant'Agostino and turning to the right is Via Sant'Agata, a rather steep descent at the bottom of which is the CHURCH OF ST. JOSEPH. Adjacent is the ARCH OF ST. JOSEPH (Arco di San Giuseppe; see fig. 45) from where a picturesque view of the Torre del Mangia can be enjoyed. The Church was built by the Corporation of carpenters in 1522 probably to Baldassarre Peruzzi's design. In 1786 it was given to the « Contrada dell'Onda » (Wav). The fine brick facade and cupola were built by Benedetto Giovannelli in 1643. Opposite Via Sant'Agata, (on the left leaving Prato di Sant'Agostino) is Via delle Cerchia which leads to Piano dei Mantellini where, right opposite the ARCH OF ST. LUCY (Arco di Santa Lucia), is the little CHURCH OF ST. NICHOLAS AND ST. LUCY. This building dates back to the year 1398 but was restored in the late years of the 16th. century. It has but one nave and a richly decorated vault due to Ventura Salimbeni and Francesco Vanni. On the right altar, placed within a tabernacle is the *Head of the Virgin*, and a seventeenth century copy of the fragment still visible of Simone Martini's fresco on the walls of the Antiporto di Camollia (the porch outside Porta Camollia). On the high altar, within a niche is a polychrome terracotta representing St. Lucy, by Giacomo Cozzarelli.

Coming out of the Church walk along Piano dei Mantellini where are the belfry and left side of the CHURCH OF SANTA MARIA DEL CARMINE, with a delightful cloister (from here the spires of the Cathedral can be seen). This building belongs to the 14th. century, but was restored in 1517 probably to Baldassare Peruzzi's design. The facade has a ridged roof, the side wall four ogival single windows, the belfry is quadrangular.

The door on the left side of the building leads into the NAVE which is single with bare beams, a wide ogival arch spanning the presbitery and fine stained glasses. Starting from the bottom of the nave, on the right wall is the *Adoring Shepherds,* by Ventura Salimbeni. First altar : the *Assumption of Mary*, a fragment of a fresco very likely by some artist of the school of Paolo di Giovanni Fei. Second altar : *St. Michael*, by Beccafumi, a very

SIMONE MARTINI (Siena, 1283-1344)

Madonna col Bambino (in deposito nella Pinacoteca)
La Vierge à l'Enfant (en dépôt à la Pinacothèque)
Madonna and Child (Deposited with the Art Gallery)
Jungfrau mit dem Sohne (Leihgabe der Pinakothek)

VI.

powerful figure in a glaring, dazzling light. Next come the *remains of two frescoes* (the first is supposed to be Ambrogio Lorenzetti's *Annunciation*). Then comes the Chapel of the Sacrament with Lorenzo Marrina's sculptured altar and Sodoma's picture representing the *Eternal Father and the Birth of Virgin Mary*. On the right wall, by the high altar is *the Madonna dei Mantellini, a panel belonging* to the Sienese-Byzantine school (about the year 1240) surrounded with figures of *Saints* due to the mastery of Francesco Vanni. The high altar has a very fine 16th. century marble ciborium. In the quire is treasured the *Madonna del Carmine*, a very precious and venerated Byzantine panel. Against the left wall, near the door is the altar with Girolamo del Pacchia's *Ascension*.

Coming out of the Church, right opposite stands PALAZZO POLLINI, once Celsi, now the property of the Neri family (no. 37); it is a very simple but extremely harmonic 16th. century building due to Baldassarre Peruzzi.

[Walking up the little hill called Via San Quirico, along the right side of Palazzo Pollini remark, on the left, the ORATORY OF SANT'ANSANO which was very likely the first baptistery built in Siena during the 9th. century, restored in 1425 and consecrated in 1443. The tower (called torre della Rocchetta) belongs to the Roman period and is generally accepted as the prison where Ansano the apostle of Siena dwelt. Inside the Church are some frescoes ascribed to Vecchietta. Along the same Via di San Quirico is the CHURCH OF SAN QUIRICO AND SANTA GIULIETTA rebuilt by Ottavio Preziani in 1598. The portal is a good 13th. century work; inside are treasured some interesting paintings of the 16th. century. Following Via Tommaso Pendola which is right in front of the Church of Sant'Ansano the visitor will find himself back to Prato di Santo Agostino. Along this street are: the two ASYLUMS FOR THE DEAF AND DUMB; the one on the right hand side contains some frescoes by Bernardino Fungai. Half way down the street is the Church of the « Contrada della Pantera » (of the Panther), called the CHURCH OF SANTA MARGHERITA (St. Margaret); it contains a wooden statue of the *Madonna and Child* of the school of Jacopo della Quercia. Next to it is the Church of the « Contrada della Tartuca » (of the Tortoise), called the CHURCH OF ST. ANTONY ABBOT (CHIESA DI S. ANTONIO ABATE). This old building was re-consecrated in the year 1684. It contains the portrait of Caterina Vannini painted by Francesco Vanni. Caterina Vannini (1562-1606) was a Sienese penitent who corresponded with Cardinal Federico Borromeo. At the bottom of the street, on the left corner is a LITTLE FOUNTAIN BELONGING TO THE CONTRADA, made in 1951 by Bruno Buracchini to celebrate the anniversary of the Patron Saint on June 13th. On that day it is the habit of the people to baptise all the children born within the limits of the Contrada during the year. Turning to the right at the bottom of Via Tommaso Pendola one goes into Via San Pietro, and then again to Sant'Agostino [see page 124].

Right opposite the above mentioned Palazzo Pollini in Piano dei Mantellini another street branches off called Via della Diana. At the junction of this street with Via S. Marco, a few steps further down, stands the little Church of the MADONNA DEL ROSARIO (the Madonna of the Rosary) with its pretty eighteenth century facade. Going back to the same Palazzo Pollini through Via San Marco, on the right hand side behind an iron gate is the CHIESA DI SAN PIETRO E PAOLO (the Church of St. Peter and St. Paul), belonging to the « Contrada della Chiocciola » (of the Snail). It was built by Flaminio del Turco with a little brick portico in front of the facade. It has the shape of a Greek cross with three very richly decorated stucco altars. Over the right altar, within a tabernacle, is the *Madonna del Rosario* (usually curtained) belonging to the late years of the 13th. century. Over the left altar is the *Conversion of St. Paul*, by Astolfo Petrazzi. Over the high altar is the *Coronation of the Virgin*, by A. Brescianino. The walls are hung with the coats-of-arms of the Protectors of the « Contrada della Chiocciola » (of the Snail).

Once back to Piano dei Mantellini, past the Chiesa del Carmine, beyond the arch called ARCO DELLE DUE PORTE there is Via Stalloreggi. The ARCO DELLE DUE PORTE (of the two Gates) is a primitive 11th. century construction in the walls of the town; on the right wall near the arch there is a 14th. century fresco of the school of Duccio di Buoninsegna representing the *Madonna and Holy Child;*

it was restored in 1954. Via Stalloreggi is a very old street with severe mediaeval buildings. HOUSE no. 89 is where DUCCIO DI BUONINSEGNA painted his famous « *Maestà* » (see the epigraph); on the corner of Via di Castelvecchio is Sodoma's fresco « *Pietà* », called by the people *la Madonna del Corvo* (the Madonna of the Raven) because a legend tells us that one of the ravens that brought the plague to Siena in the year 1348, fell down dead on that spot. A few steps further down is Piazza Postierla from where, through Via di Città, the visitor reaches once more Piazza del Campo.

Fig. 46 - Picture Gallery - 104, Bartolo di Fredi:
The Adoration of the Magi.

Itinerary IV

*FROM PIAZZA DEL CAMPO TO
SANTA MARIA DEI SERVI*

(San Cristoforo - San Donato - San Francesco -
The Oratory of St. Bernardine - San Pietro a Ovi-
le - Santa Maria di Provenzano - The State
Archives - San Martino - Santa Maria dei Servi -
Santo Spirito).

From Piazza del Campo the Vicolo di San Pietro and,
on the right, Via Banchi di Sopra lead to Piazza Tolomei where there is a pillar bearing a metal she-wolf sculptured by Domenico Arrighetti nicknamed Cavedone in
1610. On the left side of the little square stands PALAZ-
ZO TOLOMEI (fig. 47) the oldest Gothic mansion in Siena
belonging to a private citizen. It was built during the
early years of the 13th. century and restored soon after
the year 1267. It is made of stone and has two orders
of rectangular double windows (the upper order smaller
than the lower) surmounted with blind pointed arches
decorated with lobes. Opposite this palace is the 13th.
century CHURCH OF SAN CRISTOFORO (St. Cristopher) where the Council of the Republic used to hold
meetings before the Palazzo Pubblico (Town Hall) was
completed. Originally it was romanesque but was entirely rebuilt in 1779 to Tommaso Paccagnini's design.
The outside is brick, with a timpanum, four butresses
and two niches one with the statue of Blessed Bernardo Tolomei (1272-1348), the other with that of Blessed
Nera Tolomei (1220-1280), both by Giuseppe Silini.

INSIDE there is a single nave resting on four arches,
a cupola and a little transept. Right wall, second altar :
a 14th. century wooden *Crucifix* covered with leather
Third arch : a panel by Sano di Pietro representing. *St.
George killing the Dragon.* High altar : a marble group
sculptured by Bartolomeo Mazzuoli in the 18th. century
representing *Blessed Bernardo Tolomei in Glory.* Placed
in a niche in the right transept is a 15th. century ter-

racotta representing San Galgano. In the left transept a fresco has recently been discovered the authorship of which is doubtful. Left wall : over the altar is the *Madonna and Holy Child with San Luca and San Romualdo*, by Girolamo del Pacchia in 1508.

On the left hand side of the Church (Via del Moro) there is a very peculiar CLOISTER of the 12th. century (restored in 1921) from where the apse of the Church can be seen with the tombstone of Deo di Cecco Angiolieri.

On the right hand side of the Church is Via Cecco Angiolieri with the house of the homonymous witty satirical poet (on the left); opposite is a fine 13th. century stone building with pointed arches over the windows and a high tower (now « Albergo Toscana »).

Now walk along Via Banchi di Sopra. Just before the arch called ARCO DEI ROSSI, on the right is PALAZZO BICHI RUSPOLI (no. 66), now the seat of the Banca Nazionale dell'Agricoltura (National Bank of Agriculture);

Fig 47 - Palazzo Tolomei. The facade.

Fig. 48 - The Church of Santa Maria di Provenzano.

Fig. 49 - Piazza Salimbeni.

it is a two storey building of bossed stone with two ancient battlemented towers one on each side. The building no. 80 is the Gothic PALAZZO CINUGHI; it is made of brick, three storeys high with two rows of double windows. Almost opposite is PALAZZO GORI PANNILINI (now the seat of Hotel Continentale) built by Giovanni Fontana in 1577. Next comes a little square called PIAZZA SALIMBENI (fig. 49) with Sallustio Bandini's monument, the economist, sculptured by Tito Sarrocchi in 1882. On three sides are monumental buildings; the one at the bottom is PALAZZO SALIMBENI, a stone building three storeys high which dates back to the 14th. century, enlarged and restored in 1872 by Giuseppe Partini. The middle floor is decorated with six delightful three-fold windows surmounted with ogive arches with the coats-of-arms of noble families. The cornice under the roof rests on round arches supported by pedestals and bears the battlements which are decorated with four-lobed panels. On the right side of the square is PALAZZO SPANNOCCHI a Renaissance building designed by Giuliano da

Maiano (1473) and completed in the part looking on to the square in 1880 by Giuseppe Partini. It is of bossed stone, three storeys high, each storey separated from the other by a cornice; it has two rows of double windows (nine to each row, five facing Banchi di Sopra) surmounted with round arches and timpanums. Beneath the roof are medallions with busts. During the last period of the life of the Republic Piero Strozzi lived there, the brave but unlucky captain of the Sienese troops (see the inscription). On the left side of the square is PALAZZO TANTUCCI, a Renaissance building by Riccio in 1548. It is three storeys high decorated with stone elements.

These three palaces are now the seat of the bank called MONTE DEI PASCHI the important Institute of credit founded in 1624 and so called because all the banking transactions were carried out with the warrant of the Sienese « Magistrato » (Magistracy) called « Magistrato dei Paschi or Pascoli di Maremma ».

This Institute has a very good collection of tapestries, wood carvings, bronze and wrought iron decorations besides some relics of great interest for the history of Italian credit, such as: seals, parchments, old manuscripts and registers. A good collection of pictures is also ranged within the rooms: la *Madonna della Misericordia* painted by Benvenuto di Giovanni, *San Bernardino e Santa Caterina da Siena; Sant'Antonio da Padova e Santa Lucia* by Bernardino Fungai, *Salomè (Trasporto del corpo di San Giovanni)* by Domenico Beccafumi, a *Madonna with San Girolamo e il Battista* by Giacomo Pacchiarotti, « *Pietà* » by Lorenzo Rustici, a *Madonna* by Raffaello Vanni, *Giuseppe ebreo in Egitto* by Francesco Vanni, « *Pietà* » by Arcangelo Salimbeni; *Santa Caterina d'Alessandria,* sculpture by Piero d'Angelo, *Bacco* by Antonio Federighi. Among the painters of the past century and recent works of art are: *La partita a scacchi* by Luigi Mussini, a *Bishop* by Cesare Maccari, *the Sienese country-side in Spring* by Roberto Corsini, the *Sienese country-side in Autumn* by Dario Neri. Sculptures: a *Portrait* by Giovanni Duprè, the *Middle Ages* by Patrizio Fracassi, *the Seasons* by Federigo Martelli, *Maddalena* by Federigo Papi.

Now turn back and walk along Via Banchi di Sopra as far as the archway on the left which marks the entrance to Via dei Rossi. This road has many fine old houses: no. 28 is PALAZZO ROSSO, a restored brick building: no. 44 was once the PALAZZO DI GIUSTIZIA (the Court of Justice), a fourteenth century brick building. Opposite house no. 40 is Via dell'Abbadia from where the visitor can admire the back of Palazzo Salimbeni (ROCCA SALIMBENI); it has a central body, two lateral wings and a massive building adjoining the right wing. It is made of brick with lovely three fold windows and battlements. On the opposite little Square is the CHURCH OF SAN DONATO (once the Abbey of St. Michael transformed in 1683 by the Carmelites). The facade is ridged, half way up of stone and then of brick decorated with a fine marble rose window.

INSIDE there is a single nave, a transept and a polygonal dome. Over the altars and on the walls are pictures of the 17th. and 18th. centuries. Beneath the dome, which is with the apse the oldest part of the Church, one may enjoy a complete view of the characteristic effect of the windows, drum and polygonal cupola decorated with black white and red stripes. Right transept : over the altar a well framed picture of the *Madonna and the Holy Child,* by Girolamo del Pacchia. Left transept : over the altar are pictures by Giuseppe Nasini. On the high altar is a fine tabernacle with angels sculptured by Giuseppe Mazzuoli. In the apse is a fresco representing *St. Michael,* by Luigi Ademollo. Left wall, second altar : a fresco of the school of Simone Martini representing the *Madonna and Holy Child.*

At the bottom of Via dei Rossi, beyond the archway called ARCO DI SAN FRANCESCO is Piazza San Francesco with a splendid view of the surroundings. The group of the Madonna and Child between the statues of St. Francis and Santa Chiara high up on the arch are the work of Tino di Camaino; the Saints are of a later date than the Madonna.

THE BASILICA OF ST. FRANCIS
(Basilica di San Francesco)

This abbey was started in 1326 to Agostino di Agnolo's design over an old little Gothic church dedicated to

Fig. 50 - The Basilica of San Francesco - The facade - On the side: the Oratory of San Bernardino.

Fig. 51 - The Archbishopric - Ambrogio Lorenzetti: « Madonna del Latte » (the Nursing Madonna).

San Pietro and completed in 1475 probably to the design of Francesco di Giorgio Martini; it was restored during the Baroque period and again after fire in 1655, and then in the years 1885-92 by Giuseppe Partini. The belfry was built in 1765 to the design of Paolo Posi and the facade (fig. 50) was finished off by Vittorio Mariani and Gaetano Ceccarelli in the years from 1894--1913. The building is 86 metres long, 12 metres wide in the nave and 55 in the transept.

OUTSIDE it is made of brick and has a sober, imposing aspect. The ridged facade is enlivened with marble sculptures. The portal is gabled and decorated with statues and a high-relief in the lunette; several coats-of-arms are let into the brickwork on the facade and a very fine large rose window with the symbols of the Evangelists within a large frame is beneath the crowning gable. On the sides are seven very high narrow double windows crowned with pointed arches.

INSIDE this abbey has the shape of an Egyptian cross with a transept, a square apse, bare beams beneath the roof and a very huge single nave. A wonderful atmosphere of meditation and ecstasy emphasized by the coloured light pouring in through the beautiful stained glass windows fills the place. The walls are striped black and white and hung with the standards of the ancient Corporations of the Sienese Republic.

The remnants of two tombs of the Salimbeni family are placed one on each side of the entrance; the one on the right dates back to the 14th. century, the one on the left to the 13th.

Right wall : in the first lunette, the *Visitation and Saints* frescoed by Martino di Bartolommeo; in the large niche in the little Chapel are frescoed figures of *Saints* by some artist of the Sienese school of the 14th. century. Next to the cloister door is the tomb of the Tolomei family (13th. century). According to a legend, here lie the remains of Pia, the Sienese gentlewoman mentioned by Dante (see page 123).

The tribune of the high altar is beneath a huge ogival arch whilst the four smaller arches mark the entrance to the Chapels in the transept. In the left transept there are two Chapels facing the high altar.

Right transept : at the beginning : a statue of *St. Francis* of the school of Giovanni Pisano. In the second Chapel on the right hand side of the tribune is the tomb of *Cristoforo Felici* sculptured by Urbano da Cortona in 1462. Over the altar in the first Chapel is a panel of the *Madonna and Holy Child*, by Andrea Vanni. The tribune of the high altar : the very fine stained glasses of the fourfold windows are modern, produced by Zettler in Monaco; many of the stained glasses are by the same artist but some are by De Matteis of Florence. On the left wall, contained within medallions are the portraits of *Vittoria Forteguerri and Silvio Piccolomini,* Pope Pius II's parents. Left transept: first Chapel on the left side of the altar : *the Crucifixion* a detached fresco painted by Pietro Lorenzetti about the year 1331. The arrangement of the figures and their expression echo Giotto. It is a most sorrowful scene; the women among whom Mary is prostrated, the soldiers beating their breasts in self accusation, the angels with wide open arms are desperate. Third Chapel on the right wall : a detached fresco by Ambrogio Lorenzetti representing *S. Ludovico d'Angiò in front of Pope Boniface VIII.* On the left wall is another of Ambrogio Lorenzetti's frescoes representing the *Martyrdom of six Franciscan friars at Ceuta* (both rather spoilt). Fourth Chapel on the left wall : a fresco of the school of Lorenzetti representing *the Madonna and the Holy Child.* On the opposite wall of the transept, the second Chapel starting from the back of the transept known as Piccolomini-Saracini or otherwise the Chapel of the Sacrament (because it treasures in a very fresh condition some sacred wafers which were stolen in 1730) has a good graffito floor made by Marrina in 1504 to the designes of Giacomo Pacchiarotti. The left wall of the nave has a little door leading to a fifteenth century Loggia with a ruined fresco by Girolamo di Benvenuto representing the *Crucifix and Saints.* The renaissance portal in the left wall leads to the adjoining Convent.

By the door in the right wall, now enter the cloister; it is square with six arches on each side, serene and harmonic. The steps leading down to it are said to contain the remains of eighteen noble Tolomei slain by as many Salimbeni at a banquet which should have been of reconciliation given at a place on a hill near Siena still now called *Malamerenda* (a word meaning : the wicked dinner party). On the left is the Gothic portal of Niccolò Petroni's Chapel, ascribed to Domenico di Agostino in 1336. The next door leads to the SEMINARY.

The wall on the left of the entrance has a very nice marble bas-relief by a disciple of Donatello's (probably Giacomo Cozzarelli) representing the *Madonna and Holy Child,* placed within a frame. On the left wall is the*Madonna and Saints,* frescoed by Lippo Vanni.

Just outside the Seminary, on the left is the ORATORY OF ST. BERNARDINE (Oratorio di San Bernardino; door-keeper at no. 22) a 15th. century building on the site where the Saint usually preached (fig. 50).

INSIDE. THE LOWER PART OF THE ORATORY is decorated with paintings of the 17th. century. Over the altar is the *Madonna and the Holy Child, St. Bartholomew and Sant'Ansano,* by Brescianino; in the niches on each side of the altar are the terracotta statues painted white representing St. Bernardine and St. Catherine (16th. century). Upstairs, in the lunette over the vestible door is a painted wooden group of the *Madonna and Child* belonging to Jacopo della Quercia's school. Over the altar in the vestible, a *Madonna* by Sano di Pietro. In the show-case on the left is a standard painted on both sides by Francesco Vanni. In the niche on the right is a delightful bas-relief of the *Madonna and Holy Child seated upon a throne between two Angels*, sculptured by Giovanni di Agostino in 1341.

THE UPPER PART OF THE ORATORY : the ceiling and the wooden walls were elegantly decorated with stucco, by Ventura di Ser Giuliano Turapilli in 1496). A series of frescoes run from the left corner of the wall facing the entrance between one pillar and the other, as follows : *San Lodovico*, by Sodoma; *the Nativity of Mary*, by Girolamo del Pacchia; the *Presentation of Mary in the Temple*, by Sodoma (remark the perspective of the colonnade) ; the *Wedding*, by Beccafumi; *St. Bernardine*, by Girolamo del Pacchia; the *Announcing Archangel Gabriel*, by Girolamo del Pacchia (the profile is extremely delicate). On the other side of the wall : the *Annunciation*, by Girolamo del Pacchia; in the middle is the *Virgin in Glory surrounded by Saints*, by Beccafumi; *St. Anthony of Padua*, by Sodoma; *the Visitation* by Sodoma; the *Translation of Mary*, by Beccafumi; the *Assumption*, by Sodoma; *St. Francis of Assisi*, by Sodoma (remark the deeply inspired expression) ; between the windows in front of the altar the *Coronation of Mary*, by Sodoma. In this Oratory is treasured the relic of St. Bernardine's Heart and the wooden tablet with the monogram of Jesus that the Saint used when preaching.

Coming out of the Oratory of St. Bernardine, through Via dei Rossi and then Via del Comune the visitor may reach the old gateway of the town called PORTA OVILE, a 14th. century building with a curtain-wall before it. On the left in Via del Comune is the ORATORY OF THE CONTRADA DEL BRUCO (silkworm) built in the style of the seventeenth century. On the altar is treasured a *Madonna* by Luca di Tommè, and many trophies of the Palio. In the nearby valley is the FONTE D'OVILE (the Fount of Ovile) built in 1262.

At about 200 metres' distance along Via Simone Martini is an eighteenth century Parish Church called SAN

FRANCESCO ALL'ALBERINO, built on the site of an ancient Chapel where, according to tradition, the Saint of Assisi on his way to Siena in 1212 thrust his stick into the ground and at once saw it turned into a leafy evergreen oak which lived till the eighteenth century. Inside there are a few remembrances of St. Francis. Coming back through Via Pian d'Ovile, on the right, the visitor reaches FONTE NUOVA (the New Fount) a brick building of the 14th. century with three pointed arches, due to Camaino di Crescentino and Sozzo di Rustichino. Now go back to Via dei Rossi and walk as far as the brief descent called Via San Pietro a Ovile which leads to the CHURCH OF SAN PIETRO A OVILE, built in the 13th. century but altered in 1753 and recently restored together with the adjoining cloister. The facade is after the Romanesque-Lombard style; the portal has a roof over it, small single windows on the sides and a central eye-window. On the arch are the remains of a fresco by Rutilio Manetti. The two little bell housings visible on the left of the cloister are but the remnants of the ancient tower.

THE INSIDE of this Church is rectangualr with a nave and two aisles. Over the altar on the right is a fine copy of Simone Martini's *Annunciation* (1333) now in the Uffizi Gallery in Florence, with *St. John the Baptist* on one side and *St. Bernardine of Siena* on the other. This painting is ascribed to Domenico di Bartolo in the 15th. century. The altar on the left of the high altar has some fine wooden statues representing the *Madonna*, and *St. John the Evangelist near the Crucifix*, sculptured by Domenico di Niccolò de' Cori and painted by Martino di Bartolommeo in 1415. Near this altar in a temporary location, is a precious *Madonna and Child* by the artist called Maestro di San Pietro a Ovile who, according to Berenson, was Ugolino Lorenzetti; he was an anonymous author a disciple both of the school of Ugolino di Nerio and of Pietro Lorenzetti (where his composite name). Works by this artist are also in the Picture Gallery. (see page 109). On the left altar is a *painted Crucifix*, by Giovanni di Paolo.

Coming out of the Church walk along Via del Giglio, on the left, and then turn to the left into Via del Moro near the little square where there is

THE CHURCH OF ST. MARY
OF PROVENZANO
(Collegiata di Santa Maria di Provenzano)

a late Renaissance building by Flaminio del Turco (1595)
to the design of the carthusian Domenico Schifardini. It
was built to honour the miraculous image of the Madonna formerly venerated in the houses belonging to Provenzano Salvani, now treasured here (fig. 48, page 133).
The white stone facade is divided into two parts by a
cornice placed like a timpanum over the portal. The ela-
borate coping also rests on a jutting cornice; the portal
and the windows are flanked with butresses and with two
niches with the statues of Saints. The cupola rests on an
octagonal drum and is finished off with a lantern.

INSIDE there is but one nave, a short transept and a
grandiose octagonal cupola.

Right wall: first altar: *San Cerbone,* by Rutilio Manetti
in 1630. The four flags on the pillars of the cupola are
trophies, three were taken from the Turks in the 17th.
and 18th. centuries and the last (the red flag on the left
pillar) from the Chinese Boxers by the Navy Officer Alessandro Bichi Ruspoli Forteguerri in 1901 (see the commemorative inscriptions). Over the altar in the right transept:
St. Catherine's Vision, by Francesco Rustici. On the richly
decorated high altar is a venerated terracotta of the 13th.
century representing the *Madonna of Provenzano,* treasured
inside a rich tabernacle supported by four angels. On both
sides of the altar, high up, facing each other are two finely carved wooden organs. On the altar in the left transept
is a marble group sculptured by Antonio Fancelli in 1639
representing the *Crucifix between Mary Magdalene and
St. John the Evangelist.* In the Sacristy are several works of
art and some of the treasures belonging to the Collegiata of
Provenzano.

In front of the Church, on the left is Via Lucherini
which turns into Via Sallustio Bandini on the left.
In a little square on the right is the CHURCH OF SAN VI-
GILIO which originally belonged to the Camaldolesi Friars
then to the Jesuits and finally to the Vallombrosani. It
is a brick building of the 18th. century with a two sto-
reyed facade and a timpanum. The inside is Baroque with
a fine ceiling divided into fifteen compartments painted
by Raffaello Vanni. Over the altars are pictures by the

same Raffaello Vanni and by Volterrano and Mattia Preti. The third altar on the right is decorated with the statues of *St. Ignatius, St. Bernardine* and *Blessed Colombini* designed by Gian Lorenzo Bernini.

Nearby, almost opposite the Church is a court-yard called CORTE DEL CASTELLARE DEGLI UGURGIERI, a very interesting mediaeval piece of architecture which was the seat of a very powerful Set (Consorteria) of merchants, knights and bankers.

[At the bottom of Via Sallustio Bandini, on the left, is a Little Church called CHIESA DI SAN GIOVANNI BATTISTA DELLA STAFFA, O IN PANTANETO. It is a 13th. century brick building with one single gable, rebuilt in 1563 to the design of Giovan Battista Pelori and restored in 1876. It contains frescoes by Rutilio Manetti, Raffaello Vanni, a few pictures by the same Raffaello Vanni and Ventura Salimbeni. Over the altar is a fine *Madonna* by Paolo di Giovanni Fei. The lane on the side of this Church leads to FONTE DI FOLLONICA (the Fount of Follonica) a 13th. century building which rests on three pointed arches].

Coming out of the Church of San Virgilio, follow the omonymous street on the left as far as where it turns into Via Banchi di Sotto, then turn again to the left. On the right hand side of this street is PALAZZO PICCOLOMINI, the best Renaissance building in Siena (fig. 55). This mansion was started in 1469 by Pietro Paolo del Porrina from Casole probably to the design of Bernardo Rossellino. It is a smooth bossed stone building two storeys high with a mezzanine and attic. The longer side has two rows of double windows (only five on the shorter side looking on to Via Rinaldini). The two storeys are separated by a cornice; the roof has a very broad eave supported by a row of ledges.

INSIDE this building are housed the STATE ARCHIVES founded in 1858 to contain the great mass of documents concerning the historical, political, civil and artistic life of the town and of its territory. On the first floor is ranged the Museum of the Archives where are collected precious parchments, imperial diplomas, Papal bulls, contracts, statutes of the Arts, dantesque mementos, letters, autographs, Boccaccio's will, and so on. On the second floor besides a collection of seals, medals, weights and measures are ranged the celebrated painted panels, called *Tavolette della Biccherna e della Gabella* which were made to be used as covers for the semi-annual account books of the Commune. In fact, *Biccherna* and *Gabella* were the Magistracies that presided over the chief financial transactions of the ancient Republic; the former controlled and administered the public resources, collected all the money due to the Republic and provided for all the expenses and public works; the latter collected taxes and other dues. The Biccherna, mentioned for the first time in 1167, lasted till the end of the 18th. century; the Gabella, from the end of the 13th. century to the year 1808.

These *tavolette* (fig. 56) were probably started by order of a friar called Ugo di San Galgano who was at that time the Camarlingo di Biccherna (1258). They are decorated with the portraits and coats-of-arms of the administrators, allegories of political and civil life and religious scenes produced by the most eminent masters, such as Ambrogio Lorenzetti, Giovanni di Paolo, Sano di Pietro, Taddeo di Bartolo, Francesco di Giorgio Martini, Neroccio di Bartolommeo Landi, Domenico Beccafumi.

The habit of using these illustrated *tavolette* to keep the documents of the two above mentioned offices came to an end towards the middle of the 15th. century; from that time till 1682 their size was altered (they gradually became pictures to hang on the walls) and were painted even on canvas.

One hundred, more or less, of these *tavolette* are now to be seen; they are a rare and unique witness of the refined taste of the Sienese people as well as of the history and costumes of the town.

Among the most interesting miniatures treasured in the Archives is a precious piece representing the *Caleffo dell'Assunta* produced by Niccolò di Ser Sozzo Tegliacci in 1334 and another called il *Libro di Mercanzia,* painted by Sano di Pietro in 1472.

Right opposite Palazzo Piccolomini is the UNIVERSITY, very likely of the 13th. century. On the left side of the court-yard is the fine sepulchral monument to *Niccolò Aringhieri from Casole,* lecturer in Law in 1374, sculptured by an anonymous Sienese artist. The corpse is lying on the sarcophagus with the statue of *Knowledge* at his feet; on the front, the Master is portrayed holding a lesson. In the court-yard is the monument to the *Students who fell at the battle of Curtatone and Montanara* (May 29th. 1848) sculptured by Raffaello Romanelli in 1894. The

University in Siena dates from the 13th. century, but ever since the late half of the 12th. century history acquaints us with a centre of studies within the town. Further down the street there is a small square (Piazzetta) with the LOGGE DEL PAPA (the Pope's Loggia) and the Church of St. Martin. The Logge del Papa were built by order of Pope Pius II to Antonio Federighi's design in 1462, and decorated by Francesco di Giorgio Martini. They consist of three vaults in the form of a cross on round arches resting on pillars with Corinthian capitals. On the front of the building is the dedicatory inscription: « Pius II Pont. Max. gentilbus suis Piccolomineis » (*Pope Pius II to his Piccolomini relations*).

The CHURCH OF ST. MARTIN (San Martino) was built by G. Battista Pelori in 1537 but the Renaissance facade is the work of Giovanni Fontana (1613). The entrance, restored in 1962, is on top of a short double flight of steps, the facade is divided into two by a cornice; in the lower part is the portal and timpanum, in the upper two volute to link the whole to the rich coping.

INSIDE. This Church has the shape of a Latin cross, with a single nave, a short transept, a cupola a deep chancel and richly decorated marble altars. Three altars are on each side of the nave, one on each side in the transept. On the right wall of the nave, second altar: the *Circumcision,* by Guido Reni in 1640. Third altar: in a rich marble frame of Lorenzo Marrina's school (1522) is *St. Bartholomew's Martyrdom,* by Guercino. On the altar in the right transept: the statue of *St. Thomas of Villabruna,* by Giuseppe Mazzuoli; on the opposite altar is the *Conception* by the same artist in 1611. The high altar is the work of Marrina (1522); it is decorated with statues of *Angels and Saints,* by Giuseppe Mazzuoli. In the Chancel the vault, and as the cupola are richly frescoed. The stained glass window representing St. Martin is probably due to Pastorino de'Pastorini. Here are also five wooden gilt polychromic statues waiting to be definitely ranged elsewhere; they are: the *Madonna and the Holy Child,* ascribed to Jacopo della Quercia; *St. Anthony the Abbot,* to a disciple of his; *St. Bartholomew, St. Andrew and St. John the Baptist,* by Giovanni di Francesco da Imola, all produced in the lapse of time from 1419 to 1425. The third altar on the left wall of the nave was sculptured by Lorenzo Marrina; over it hangs the picture of the *Nativity*, by Domenico Beccafumi in 1523 (the colours have turned black). On the second altar are some painted wooden statues of the 15th. century : the *Crucifix, the Madonna and John the Evangelist*. Over the first altar *St. Ivone* by Raffaello Vanni. On the left just inside the door is *the Battle of Porta Camollia* (1526) by Giovanni di Lorenzo Cini.

Leaving the Church turn to the left into Vicolo delle Scotte where the GHETTO is with the SYNAGOGUE built by the Florentine Giuseppe del Rosso in 1786; it contains several works of art. On the left just outside the Church, but without turning into Vicolo delle Scotte, is Via del Porrione where, just past the side of the Church is the ARCICONFRATERNITA DELLA MISERICORDIA and the adjoining Oratory (the ancient Company of St. Anthony the Abbot, founded by B. Andrea Gallerani about the year 1250) which was the « *Ospedale dei Pellegrini* » — the Pilgrims' Hospital — till 1391. Here, over the altar is a panel of the *Virgin* ascribed to Girolamo del Pacchia; in the lunettes are paintings by Rustichino, Alessandro Casolani and Francesco Vanni; there are also two wooden statues representing the *Annunciation,* both of the 15th. century. In the entrance hall is a wooden statue of the school of Vecchietta representing *St. Anthony the Abbot*. In the assembly room are some heads of biers (1540) by Domenico Beccafumi and Guidoccio Cozzarelli, and the portrait of Bartolomeo Carosi nicknamed Brandano, the popular Sienese Prophet, by Pietro Sorri (17th. century).

Now walk along Via San Martino as far as the Piazzetta di San Giusto with the granite COLUMN of the Roman age bearing a mediaeval lantern shaped like a little cage. Go straight on to Via di San Girolamo on the right hand side of which is the CONVENT AND CHURCH OF SAN GIROLAMO, a 14th. century building decorated inside with frescoes by Girolamo del Pacchia; there is also a good picture of the *Coronation of the Virgin,* by Sano di Pietro and in the cloister the *Assumption,* by Bernardino Fungai in 1487. From Via di San Girolamo go straight on to Via dei Servi which leads to Piazza Alessandro Manzoni; in this Piazza is

THE BASILICA OF ST. MARY OF THE «SERVI»

(Basilica di Santa Maria dei Servi)

a 13th. building enlarged in the years from 1473 to 1528. The facade is unfinished; two rose windows, however, are visible one just marked out, the other open. The lovely bell tower with single windows in the lower part increasing to four-fold windows on the top, all resting on pointed arches, is Romanesque (13th. century) but restored in 1926 together with the rest of the Basilica (fig. 52).

THE INTERIOR is magnificent, serene and harmonic; it has the shape of a Latin cross with the nave separated from the aisles by two rows of five granite pillars (fig. 53). The style is mixed: Gothic in the transept, and in the apse (restored), Renaissance in the nave and aisles. The latter were probably designed by Baldassarre Peruzzi

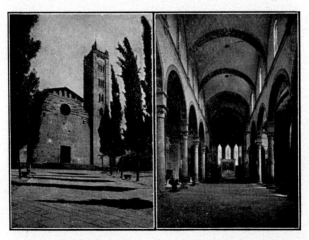

Fig. 52 - The Basilica of Santa Maria dei Servi - Outside.

Fig. 53 - The Basilica of Santa Maria dei Servi - Inside.

Fig. 54 - S. María dei Servi - Pietro Lorenzetti: *The Massacre of
the Innocents.*

and built by Ventura Turapilli. Next to the first pillar on
the right is a fine holy water stoup some of the parts of
which are of the 13th. century.

On the wall of the right aisle, next to the first Chapel
are the remains of a fresco of the 14th. century. Second
altar: the *Madonna and Holy Child called the Madonna
del Bordone,* by Coppo di Marcovaldo in 1261, partially
re-painted by a disciple of Duccio's; this work shows marked Byzantine reminiscences (the author was taken a prisoner at the battle of Monteaperti and painted this picture
as his ransom). Third altar: the *Birth of Mary* by Rutilio
Manetti. Fifth altar: the *Massacre of the Innocents,* by
Matteo di Giovanni, a scene full of movement (see page
125); in the lunette is one of the best canvases by the
now mentioned artist, the *Madonna and Saints* (1491). Delightful is the chromatic harmony, the graceful forms and
gentle expression. On the right wall is the *Adoring Shep-*

herds, by Taddeo di Bartolo in 1404. In the right transept over the Sacristy door the *Madonna and Child* by Segna di Bonaventura, plainly inspired by the art of Duccio.
Two Chapels are on both sides of the high altar in the
transept. Behind the high altar are three-lobed windows
with stained glasses.

Right transept, the second Chapel on the right side of
the high altar : the right wall is frescoed with the *Massacre of the Innocents* by Pietro Lorenzetti, rather spoilt
but still most beautiful (fig. 54). The heart-felt scene is
presented in a most dramatic way. The desperate mothers
are bent over the little corpses while a group of soldiers
brandishing their swords hold them back. In the background is a tumultuous crowd pressed forward by cavalry
soldiers with yellow standards. Houses and palaces are
behind them and on a balcony is King Herod. Over the altar in the same Chapel is the *Madonna del Popolo* (the
Madonna of the people), by Lippo Memmi, one of the most
graceful works of this clever imitator of Simone Martini.
The high altar : Bernardino Fungai's altar screen representing the *Coronation of the Virgin* (1500). Left transept, second
Chapel on the left hand side of the high Chapel : *Herod's
banquet,* by Pietro Lorenzetti (on the right) and the *Transit
of St. John the Evangelist* (on the left), both rather spoilt.
The Chapel at the bottom of the left transept : the Madonna known as the *Madonna della Misericordia* (the Madonna of Mercy) by Giovanni di Paolo ; this work is dated 1436
and signed but the signature Giovanni di Pietro is wrong.
On the wall of the left aisle, second altar : the Madonna
known as the *Madonna del Belvedere,* by Jacopo di Mino
del Pellicciaio in 1363, with the *Madonna* and *St. Joseph*
by Bernardino Fungai on the sides. First altar : the *Annunciation,* by Francesco Vanni. High up on the entrance
wall is a 14th. century *Crucifix* probably by Niccolò di
Segna.

Coming out of the Church stop to admire the lovely
view of the Torre del Mangia, the back of the Palazzo
Comunale (the Town Hall) and the right side of the Cathedral with the huge facade of the New Cathedral.

Near the Chiesa dei Servi, a little further down, in
Via Val di Montone is the ORATORY OF THE HOLY
TRINITY (ring for the door keeper at number eleven)
built in 1298 by B. Francesco Patrizi and restored
towards the end of the 16th. century. This little place is
sumptuously decorated with stucchi and wooden carvings by Prospero da Brescia and the Sienese Rusticone.

and with frescoes of the 17th century. On the entrance wall: the *Victory of Clodoveus over Alaric II* by Raffaello Vanni (1652).

THE INTERIOR. The four large pictures and the ten smaller ones are the work of Giuseppe Nasini; they illustrate the *Historical Vicissitudes of the Catholic Church* and *scenes from the life of Blessed Giovanni Piccolomini* (1696-98). In the vaults are the figures of *Saints* and in the five lunettes above the cornice *St. John's Vision of the Apocalypse*, all by Ventura Salimbeni (1595-1602). The tribune of the altar was produced by Giuseppe Nasini, Ventura Salimbeni, Astolfo Petrazzi and Alessandro Casolani. The bronze *Crucifix* over the altar was modelled by Prospero da Brescia and cast by Alessandro Vannini in 1579. Inside the Chapel is the *Madonna and Holy Child* by Sano di Pietro and in the Sacristy the *Madonna and Holy Child with St. Michael and St. John the Baptist*, by Neroccio di Bartolommeo Landi.

At the bottom of the steps just outside the Oratory runs Via Roma where is the Church of the old Monastery of Santa Maria degli Angeli (no longer existent) called of the SANTUCCIO, started in 1362. The facade however was finished off in 1557 to the design of Annibale Bichi. It contains two wooden statues of the *Annunciation* ascribed to Giovanni di Turino. Nearby is the seat of the SOCIETA DI ESECUTORI DI PIE DISPOSIZIONI (the Society for the Execution of Pious Dispositions) where several good works of art are treasured among which Benvenuto di Giovanni's picture of *St. Catherine going back to Rome with Pope Gregory XI*, a Reliquary in the form of a triptych very likely by Bernardino Fungai, a tabernacle produced by Ugolino di Nerio and paintings by Niccolò di Ser Sozzo Tegliacci, Sodoma, and Giacomo Cozzarelli.

[At the bottom of Via Roma is the gate of the town called PORTA ROMANA with a curtain wall, built by Agnolo di Ventura in 1327. There are still to be seen the remains of a fresco which was ruined during the last War; it represented the *Coronation of Mary* and had been painted by Taddeo di Bartolo (1417) Sassetta (1447) and Sano di Pietro (1459). Beneath the arch are still some of Sassetta's *Angels*].

On the left hand side of Via Roma is Via del Refugio; in the little Piazzetta on the right is the CHURCH OF THE REFUGIO, a building started in 1598 to Benedetto Giovannelli's design with a late Renaissance facade (17th. century). It contains paintings by Francesco Vanni, Domenico di Bartolo, Vecchietta, some very fine sacred vestments and goldsmiths' works of the 16th. and 17th. centuries.

Still in Via Roma, at no. 47 is the PALAZZO DI SAN GALGANO built in a style resembling that of Giuliano da Maiano (about the year 1474; see page 134-135). The smooth bossed facade has two rows of five double windows. On the corner of this street with Via dell'Oliviera is the COLONNA DEL PONTE (the column of the Bridge) bearing a stone she-wolf and a wrought iron bracket (1470). On the corner against, the old walls of the town, is a fountain which was built in the year 1221. Now enter Via di Pantaneto by the gateway called PORTA DEL PONTE DI ROMANA (it is the old Arch of San Maurizio decorated with a fresco by Bernardo Capitelli (1618) representing *Trinity and Saints*). The first turning on the right is Via dei Pispini where is the CHURCH OF THE HOLY SPIRIT (Chiesa di Santo Spirito) a brick Renaissance building which dates back to 1498. The facade is ridged, the portal has a timpanum, probably designed by Baldassare Peruzzi in 1519, high up is a rose window and coping; the sides are supported by massive buttresses; the huge dome is due to Giacomo Cozzarelli (1508).

INSIDE this church there is a single nave restored of late. Just inside the entrance behind a gate on the right is the *Crib;* some of the painted terracotta statues were produced by Fra Ambrogio della Robbia in 1509. The first Chapel on the right is called the Cappella degli Spagnoli (the Spaniards' Chapel) decorated in 1530 by Sodoma with pictures representing *San Niccolò da Tolentino,* on the left, *Archangel Michael* on the right, *the Virgin giving Alfonso the robes of the Dominican Order* in the lunette; he painted also the frescoes, as follows: *St. Sebastian* on the left, *St. Anthony the Abbot* on the right, *San Giacomo di Compostella trampling upon the defeated Saracens* in the lunette. In the second Chapel is a wooden statue by Giacomo Cozzarelli representing *San Vincenzo Ferreri.* The left wall of the third Chapel is decorated with *the Coronation of Mary,* by Domenico Beccafumi. Over the altar in the fourth Chapel is *San Giacinto in Gloria*, by Francesco Vanni; on the walls are scenes from the life of *San Giacinto*, by Ventura Salimbeni. A very bright fresco by Giuseppe Nasini is painted on the wall of the apse representing *Pentecost*; on the lateral pillars by the altar are four figures of *Saints*, by Rutilio Manetti. Facing each other high up on the wall are two simple but very elegant chantries.

Over the altar in the third Chapel on the left side is the *Coronation of Mary*, by Girolamo del Pacchia and on the right wall is a painted wooden *Crucifix* made by Sano di Pietro. The two wooden statues on the sides of the altar represent the *Holy Virgin* and *St. Jerome* and are ascribed to Giacomo Cozzarelli. The second Chapel contains a wooden statue of *St. Catherine of Siena*, by Giacomo Cozzarelli. The first Chapel is decorated with a very pleasant picture of the *Assunta and Saints*, by Matteo Balducci in 1509. Remark the rhythm of the central group, the Virgin's sweet expression and the decorative design of the wings of the Angels. Inside the cloister of the once Dominican Convent, a very noble construction, is

Fig. 55 - Palazzo Piccolomini, now the seat of the State Archives.

Fig. 56 - A panel painted for a book belonging to the Hospital.

a scene of the *Crucifixion* painted by Fra Paolino da Pistoia in 1516.

[On the little square in front of the Church is the FOUNTAIN OF PISPINI (1534). Walking down Via dei Pispini the visitor will soon find the CHURCH OF SANTA CHIARA situated just after the ORATORIO DI SAN GAETANO in the « Contrada del Nicchio » (Shell); the Romanesque facade was destroyed during the last war. At the end of Via dei Pispini is the gate of the town called PORTA PISPINI, othervise « *di San Viene* » so called because in the year 1107 the relics of Ansano, the early martyr, entered the town by this gate amid the joyious exclamations of the people : « il Santo viene... Il Santo viene... » (The Saint is coming... The Saint is coming...). It is believed that the body of the Saint was found by a sheperdess near the river Arbia. In 1326 the tower (torrione) was built, probably by Minuccio di Rinaldo, later on decorated by Sodoma with a fresco representing the *Nativity* (1531); the scene shows splendid figures of Angels singing hosannas. The little fortress on the left hand side of the gateway was built by Baldassare Peruzzi].

From the corner of Via dei Pispini turning to the right into Via Pantaneto very soon appears the facade of the CHIESA DI SAN GIORGIO (by Pietro Cremoni in 1741) which in olden times was the church of the Cavalry Militia. It is made of travertine with two heavy columns and projecting butresses, Corinthian capitals and an uneven cornice running round the timpanum. The steeple is Romanesque (1260) with thirty-eight windows which are believed to stand for the military Companies at the battle of Monteaperti. Inside this Church is the tomb of Francesco Vanni, the painter (1563-1610). The picture of the *Crucifixion* by Francesco Vanni himself is treasured here; over the high altar is *St. George* by Sebastiano Conca. At the end of Via Pantaneto, on the side of Palazzo Piccolomini is Via Rinaldini which leads back to Piazza del Campo.

Itinerary V

FROM PIAZZA DEL CAMPO TO PORTA CAMOLLIA

(Fontebranda - Sanctuary and House of St. Catherine - Basilica of San Domenico - Library of the Intronati - Archeological Museum - Fontegiusta - Porta Camollia).

From Piazza del Campo go to Via di Città through the Vicolo (lane) di San Paolo, turn to the left and then to the right into Via delle Terme which leads to PIAZZA DELL'INDIPENDENZA. On the left side of this Piazza is the TEATRO DELL'ACCADEMIA DEI ROZZI (the theatre of the « Rozzi » Academy), built in 1816 to Alessandro Doveri's design restored in 1874 by Augusto Corbi and now being repaired; on the right is the LOGGIA DELL'INDIPENDENZA built by Archimede Vestri in 1887; behind is the red brick battlemented PALAZZO BALLATI and a huge rectangular stone tower.

Turn into Via Diaceto on the left side of the Piazza; after a few steps the visitor may enjoy a very pretty view of the quarters of the Town called Fontebranda with the Basilica of San Domenico, looking almost like a fortress. After that turn to the right into Via della Galluzza which is still one of the most picturesque mediaeval streets of the town spanned by arches with huge ancient buildings on either sides; the first arch has a delightful threefold window. Follow the steep lane called Costaccino and then turn to the left into Via di Fontebranda (here is another superb view of the Basilica of San Domenico) and walk down to the bottom where the font called FONTEBRANDA is (this region draws its name, so it seems, from a house that belonged to a certain Brando or Ildebrando, or maybe to the old Brandi family). The building already existed in 1081, it was enlarged in 1188 by Bellarmino and restored in 1486

Fig. 57 - Fontebranda and the Basilica of San Domenico.

by Giovanni di Stefano. It is made of brick and has three huge ogival arches surmounted with as many pointed spandrels. The roof is crowned with battlements resting partly on a row of little arches with triangular ledges. On the walls are four waterspouts in the form of lions (fig. 57). The green transparent water is very prettily reflected on the vaults. Opposite, higher up, is the ruddy massive rock-like absidal part of the Church of San Domenico.

Walk along the narrow lane called Via del Tiratoio on the right of Fontebranda, pass the little porch just near, and again on the right you will at once find the entrance to

THE SANCTUARY AND HOUSE
OF ST. CATHERINE
(Santuario e Casa di Santa Caterina)

the place sacred (together with the Basilica of San Domenico) to the memory and worship of the Patroness of Italy. (For the door keeper ring the bell on the door of the opposite house).

Here lived Caterina Benincasa (March 25th., 1347 - April 29th, 1380) the daughter of Jacopo the dyer, one of the members of the « Arte della Lana » (the wool Guild) and of Monna Lapa di Puccio Piagenti. She was a woman of superior intelligence - and a very clever writer with a grand style and deep faith - inspired with an irresistible mystic force. But her mysticism was constructive, almost pugnacious and inspired the humblest and most obscure deeds as well as the greatest enterprises. She suceeded in bringing Pope Gregory XI back to Rome from Avignon where he lived as a captive in the year 1377. In 1461 she was canonized by the Sienese Pope Pius II and in 1939 proclaimed the Patroness of Italy by Pope Pius XII.

Soon after her canonization the Sienese expressed their veneration by consecrating the Saint's House and turning it into a Sanctuary. The original plan of the house was changed and, a few years ago, after many interruptions the works started in the 15th. century were at last completed.

The Lower Oratory was created on the site where once was the dye shop of Catherine's father; it was started in 1465 and completed at the beginning of the 17th century. The upper Oratory (once the kitchen) was started in 1496 and completed at the end of the 16th. century. The Chiesa del Crocifisso (the Church of the Crucifix) of the early years of the 17th. century, was built on the site where once was the kitchen garden; the Oratorio della Cameretta, on the site where was the Saint's room. All these rooms were decorated with paintings during the past century. The porch that joins the Chiesa del Crocifisso to the Upper Oratory, once ascribed to Baldassarre Peruzzi, is now believed to be the work of G. B. Pelori in 1533. The double outside loggia called the Porch of the Communes of Italy was built in homage to the Patron Saint by the whole Nation (see fig. 58) and was completed in 1941.

On the architrave over the door of the Saint's House is written: « Sponsæ Kristi Catherinæ domus ».

THE UPPER ORATORY. The floor is covered with 3061 majolica tiles produced in the 17th. century by Girolamo di Marco, the potter of Pantaneto (this floor is usually covered up). Against the walls are pillars decorated with gilt stucco work. The fine coffered ceiling was restored in 1594 to the design of Riccio. Beneath the altar a piece of the old fire place and sooty wall can still be seen.

The panel on the altar represents *the Stigmata of St. Catherine* and was painted by Bernardino Fungai; all around are paintings by Riccio. Over the precious Renaissance stalls are the following pictures : starting from the left side of the altar, *Jesus showing the Saint a Cross she had given to a poor beggar* (of the school of Sodoma). On the left wall : *Blessed Ambrogio Sansedoni*, by Gaetano Marinelli in 1865; *The Condemned converted by the Saint's prayers,* by Lattanzio Bonastri di Lucignano in 1589; *the Saint's Communion,* by Pomarancio, *the Saint rids a possessed woman,* by Pietro Sorri; *Blessed Giovanni Colombini,* by Alessandro Casolani. On the wall opposite the altar : *Jesus exchanging his heart with that of the Saint,* attributed to Francesco Vanni; over this picture there is another representing *the Saint Illuminated by the Holy Ghost,* by Rutilio Manetti. In the concave lunette is *the Canonization of the Saint,* one of the best works by Francesco Vanni; at the side of this painting is *the Saint receiving from Jesus a crown of thorns,* by Francesco Vanni and over it is *the Saint's vision of Jesus bound to the pillar,* by Manetti; Right wall: *Blessed Andrea Gallerani,* by Francesco Vanni; *the Saint persuading the people of Rome to be faithful to Pope Urbano VI,* by Casolani; *Gregory XI brings the Seat of Papacy back to Rome,* by Pomarancio; *the Mystic Nuptials of St. Catherine,* by Arcangelo Salimbeni in 1579; *St. Bernardine,* by Pietro Aldi in 1865; on the right side of the altar is a picture of *the Saint offering her gown to a beggar,* belonging to the school of Sodoma. At the bottom of the church is the CHIESA DEL CROCIFISSO (the Church of the Crucifix) erroneously ascribed to G.B. Pelori. It has the shape of a Latin cross with a single nave and draws its name from the fact that in 1623 the Crucifix (ascribed to Giunta Pisano) before which Saint Catherine received the Stigmata (1375) was placed there after having been stolen from the Church of Santa Cristina in Pisa (at present the holy relic is

Fig. 58 - The Porch of the Communes of Italy in front of St. Catherine's House. In the backround is the Basilica of San Domenico.

Fig. 59 - The House of St. Catherine of Siena.

treasured in the altar). The style is baroque; the vault is frescoed by Giuseppe Nasini with *the Glory St. Catherine* and the walls by Niccolò Franchini, Alessio Calvi, Galgano Perpignani, and Liborio Guerrini. On the sides of the altar are works by Nasini and on the walls by several authors of the 18th. century. Right transept; over the altar : the *Apotheosis of the Saint,* by Rutilio Manetti; over the opposite altar is *St. Catherine and Gregory XI,* by Sebastiano Conca. Leaving the Church go down to the ORATORIO DELLA CAMERA (the Oratory built over the Saint's room) where the Saint preferred to live and pray and receive her visitors. The coffered ceiling is gilt, the walls are frescoed by Alessandro Franchi (1896) with scenes from the *Life of the Saint.* Over the altar within a precious frame is the picture of *the Stigmata of St. Catherine,* painted by Girolamo di Benvenuto. In the adjoining room is the now closed window through which the Saint used to distribute alms, the stone that was her pillow (beneath the grating) her lantern, a little bottle of aromas she used when visiting the sick and a fragment of the stick she took with her to France (in a reliquary). In a corner is the statue of the *Saint praying* by Pietro Repossi in 1940. Down below is the LOWER ORATORY otherwise called the ORATORIO DI SANTA CATERINA IN FONTEBRANDA (the Oratory of St. Catherina in Fontebranda) or even ORATORIO DELLA CONTRADA DELL'OCA (Oratory of the Contrada of the Goose) ; it was once the ground floor of Benincasa's shop. It has a single nave with two cruciform vaults (1473). On the altar is a painted wooden statue of *St. Catherine,* carved by Neroccio di Bartolommeo Landi in 1474; the expression is very good.

Over the lunette are the following frescoes : low down, *five Angels* by Sodoma; higher up, *the Saint's Stigmata,* by Girolamo del Pacchia. The walls, too, are frescoed, as follows : right wall starting from the altar, *the Corpse of St. Agnes of Montepulciano lifts a foot for St. Catherine to kiss,* by Girolamo del Pacchia; *Dominicans assaulted by Brigands are set free thanks to the Saint's prayers,* also by Girolamo del Pacchia. The wall facing the altar : *the Saint at the Consistory,* by Sebastiano Folli; on one side is represented the *Saint in Florence* and on the other the *Saint on her way back from Florence.* Left wall : *the recovery of Matteo Cenni from the Plague,* by Girolamo del Pacchia and *the Florentine Soldiers sent to kill the Saint are becoming blind,* by Ventura Salimbeni. Beneath this Oratory in the basement of the house is the miraculous « cellar » where the Saint used to keep her inexhaustible barrel of water.

AMBROGIO LORENZETTI (Siena, ...1318-1348)

La « *Madonna del Latte* » (Seminario)
Madone « *du Lait* » (Séminaire)
The Madonna « *of the Milk* » (Seminary)
« *Madonna del Latte* » (Seminar)

VII.

In the hall adjoining the Sacristy of the Lower Oratory (1902) is ranged the Museum of the « Contrada dell'Oca » (the Contrada of the Goose).

Leaving the Sanctuary stop to admire the facade of the Church by Francesco di Duccio del Guasta and Corso di Bastiano in 1474. In the lunette over the portal is *St. Catherine among Angels,* by Urbano da Cortona (fig. 59).

Now walk up Via di Santa Caterina and turn to the left into Costa di Sant'Antonio, a steep hill with a good view of the Loggia of the Sanctuary; just after it there is a low brick archway leading to the Piazza where is

THE BASILICA OF ST. DOMINIC
(Basilica di San Domenico)

a very severe and imposing brick building in the monastic Gothic style (fig. 57, page 155) started in 1225 by the Dominican Friars who, according to the Cistertian models, planned the rectangular nave and bare beamed roof, and carried out the work through several successive periods of time (1254). After an interruption which lasted almost half a century the back part of the temple was enlarged, that is, the part facing Fontebranda. Then the transept was built the lower part of which (once the Church of San Gregorio; 12th. century) formed the CRYPT but it was so large and grandiose that it assumed the aspect of a Church. In fact, it was then called the «Chiesa di sotto» or else the «Chiesa dei Morti» (the Lower Church or the Church of the Dead) and was used as a burial place. The relations of Saint Catherine are buried there. In the year 1340 the graceful gabled steeple was built, but it was shortened several times in later years till it was reduced to its actual limited proportion; the gables were changed into battlements in the 18th. century. In the 14th. century, the lateral Chapels were built in the transept. In the next century the huge ogival arch connecting the head of the cross with the foot was built. During the Baroque age the adding of other altars in the nave spoilt the original aspect and the style of the temple. In 1532 the Basilica

Fig. 60 - San Domenico - Andrea Vanni: *The portrait of St. Catherine of Siena.*

suffered much damage through fire and again in 1779 through a terrible earthquake, but was partially restored by the Monks of Monte Cassino. Now the Church belongs once more to the Dominican Friars and has been restored to its original style. All the blocked up windows have been re-opened and fitted with stained glass telling the story of St. Catherine's life. The first four windows were donated by the Monte dei Paschi and are the work of Domenico Cantatore, Fabrizio Clerici, Giorgio Quaroni and Bruno Saetti.

THE OUTSIDE walls are entirely made of brick. The facade was never finished off maybe in consideration of the pre-existing Cappella delle Volte (the Chapel of the Vaults) dedicated to St. Catherine, which is the rectangular building grafted to the walls of the church. Once upon a time the little arches on the left side surmounted a row of niches containing patrician tombs. Remark the transept much higher than the nave and the apse. The huge walls are most impressive seen from the little valley of Fontebranda and resemble in style, more than any other part of the Church, the Cistertian buildings (characterized by a huge arch with rose-windows and six ogival windows). The whole lower part of the building forms the CRYPT. From the space in front of the Abbey a most peculiar and picturesque view of Siena is to be admired: in the foreground are the battlements of Fontebranda beyond which are the steep hillocks where the houses of the town are clustered, and Via di Fontebranda stretching its ribbon-like shape as far as the old gateway called Porta Salaria; it is a multi-coloured picture with different hues of red, yellow and grey. High up on the left is the bright stumpy Ballati tower, in the middle the red Mangia tower, on the right the black and white striped structure of the Cathedral with the facade of the Baptistery the left transept, the cupola with its double row of loggias and the belfry.

In the CLOISTER (1425) on the right side of the facade, which has now been almost entirely re-built, are fragments of some beautiful frescoes by Lippo Memmi and Andrea Vanni (1372). Enter the Abbey by the door on the left.

INSIDE - This Gothic Church has the shape of Egyptian cross with a single nave. Three Chapels are on each side of the high altar, and an altar is at each end of the transept.

At the bottom of the nave is the CAPPELLA DELLE VOLTE (the Chapel of the Vaults) which was restored in 1952, on two arches with cruciform vaults (from which it draws its name) and a re-built pillar against which it is traditional that St. Catherine used to lean. Here, in 1363 Catherine Benincasa entered the order of the Mantellate and here she used to linger in prayer and ecstasy (an inscription on the pillar reminds the visitor of this). At the bottom of the Chapel is the altar with the famous fresco of the Saint by her disciple Andrea Vanni which is believed to be the Saint's only portrait (fig. 60). Then, from left to right are : *St. Catherine reciting the Office with Jesus Christ*, by Crescenzio Gambarelli in 1607; *Santa Rosa sees St. Catherine in a vision* and *the Death of St. Catherine*, by Gambarelli in 1602. On the opposite wall is the *Canonization of St. Catherine*, by Mattia Preti and on the sides two pictures with scenes from Catherine's life.

On the left side of the nave, over the altars, are : *San Giacinto* by Francesco Vanni; *St. Catherine of Alessandria's nuptials'* by Alessandro Casolani; *St. Antony the Abbot recovering a possessed woman*, by Rutilio Manetti; a detached fresco of the *Virgin and Holy Babe with St. John the Baptist*, ascribed to Pietro Lorenzetti.

On the right : *The Madonna appears to Blessed Andrea Gallerani*, by Stefano Volpi in 1640; *The Nativity of Virgin Mary*, by Alessandro Casolani; Francesco di Giorgio Martini's *Crib* famous for the careful drawing, plastic beauty and space; in the lunette is Matteo di Giovanni's *Pietà* and on the altar foot-board *Stories of Saints* by Bernardino Fungai.

On the right side of the nave is the CAPPELLA DI SANTA CATERINA (St. Catherine's Chapel), built in the year 1488. Within a recently made reliquary (1940) shaped like a Gothic temple, is treasured the Saints head. Her body is in Rome in the Church of Santa Maria della Minerva. The exquisite marble tabernacle was made by Giovanni di Stefano in 1466. This Chapel is almost entirely frescoed by Sodoma. On the left side of the altar is the painter's masterpiece : *St. Catherine's Swoon* (fig. 61), famous for the figure of the Saint which almost seems to be breathing (she is portrayed leaning against the richly decorated pillar in the Cappella delle Volte); the admirable harmony of the whole group and the pretty landscape are delightful. On the right side of the altar : *St. Catherine's*

Fig. 61 - San Domenico - Sodoma: *St. Catherine's Swoon.*

Ecstasy, 1526. On the left wall: *Niccolò di Tuldo's Martyrdom*. All these works are due to the mastery of Sodoma, and so are the figures of *St. Luke* and *St. Jerome* on the arch of the entrance door. On the right wall is the scene of the *Saint recovering a possessed woman*, by Francesco Vanni in 1593. The same artist painted the portraits of *B. Tommaso Nacci Caffarini*, the Saint's secretary, and of *Raimondo da Capua*, the Saint's confessor and chief biographer. Remark the grotesques on the pillars and the graffito marble floor (16th. century). The staircase beyond the Cappella delle Volte leads down to, the *Crypt* where, on the High Altar, is Sano di Pietro's famous *Crucifix*. By the same artist is the panel of *St. Bernardine of Siena* on the left whilst the *Stories of the Rosary* are believed to be Sodoma's work. The wooden statue on the right is Vecchietta's *St. Anthony*.

THE RIGHT TRANSEPT. In the third chapel on the right side of the High Altar, left wall, *Virgin Mary, St. Catherine of Siena and St. Paul* (a 16th century work) - In the second chapel on the same side, called the Cappella dei Tedeschi (the Chapel of the Germans) are buried some German students who died in Siena during the 16th. century and the 17th. Some of the Latin epitaphs sound as a word of praise for Italian art and culture. In the first Chapel over the altar. Paolo di Giovanni Fei's *Madonna and Holy Babe*. Another *Madonna and Holy Babe* is on the right wall; the Saints are *St. John the Baptist and St. Gerome*, both by Matteo di Giovanni.

THE HIGH ALTAR has a very fine marble ciborium made by Giuliano da Maiano, the same who produced the delightful figures of the angels placed against the walls as candelabra (1475).

LEFT TRANSEPT. In the first chapel on the left of the High Altar : a *Madonna and Child* by Sano di Pietro; second chapel, right wall : *St. Barbara on a throne between St. Mary Magdalene and St. Catherine of Alexandria* (1479), a delightful picture though rather spoilt; in the lunette there is Matteo di Giovanni's *Epiphany*. On the left wall a *Madonna and Child with Saints* and above it « *Pietà* » by Benvenuto di Giovanni in 1483. On the wall opposite is Giuseppe Pianigiani's sepulchral monument made by Pietro Tenerani from Rome in 1829.

The last altar in the right arm of the cross is that of Beato Ambrogio Sansedoni; the last altar on the left is delicated to San Domenico.

Fig 62 - One of the rooms of the Museum of Archeology.

Leaving the Church of San Domenico turn to the right into Via della Sapienza. No. 5 is the BIBLIO-TECA DEGLI INTRONATI (the Library of the Intronati) founded by Archdeacon Salustion Bandini in 1759. Apply to the director to see the miniated codes, the Roman missals, a Roman pontifical with French miniatures of the 15th. century, incunabula among which Dante's *Divine Comedie* with drawings by Sandro Botticelli in 1481, the *Polifilo*, letters written by St. Catherine, some sketch books with drawings by Francesco di Giorgio Martini, Giuliano da Sangallo, Baldassarre Peruzzi, Domenico Beccafumi and others, a splendid bronze reliquary in the form of a bust with the image of St. Catherine of Siena, an antiphonary miniated by Giovanni di Paolo, a Sienese Franciscan breviary of the 15th. century miniated by Sano di Pietro, the « Book of the Hours » (Libro d'Ore) miniated by Littifredo Corbizi in 1494 and a Bizantine Gospel of the 10th. century from the Imperial Palace of Constantinoples, bound in glit silver decorated with enamel paintings, as follows: on the back, in the middle: the *Ressurrection;* on the front *the Ascension;* on the sides the figures of *Prophets and Apostles* with the *Virgin and the Holy Child.* The library has 300,000 volumes, 1000 incunabula and 6000 manuscripts.

The building marked no. 1 in Via della Sapienza is the seat of the MUSEO ARCHEOLOGICO ETRUSCO (the Etrusco Museum of Archeology), a recent building. This most interesting collection of antiquities consists essentially of the collections belonging to Bargagli, Casuccini and Chigi Zondadari (fig. 62). There are eleven rooms to visit with objects ranging from the neolithic period right through the Etruscan and Greek age down to the Roman age, some of which are of great documentary and artistic value. There are pieces which come from Chiusi, Chianciano, Montepulciano, Sarteano, Volterra, Castelluccio della Foce, Cetona and the surroundings of Siena; among them are: ossuaries, cups, buccheri, foculi, skyphoi, curved razors, fibula, spear-heads, needles, arrow tops belonging to the neolithic age, axes, bronzes cinerary urns, censers, mirrors, scent bottles, and scarabs. There are also some Etruscan urns which are peculiarly interesting (numbers 729, 730, 731, 721, 728, 734, 737), a very beautiful front piece of a Roman sarcophagus marked no. 6, amphoras, bowls, and exquisitely decorated plates.

Just after the Museum, on the corner of the street is the CHURCH OF SAN PELLEGRINO ALLA SAPIENZA, a very ancient building, which belonged to Santa Maria della Misericordia till 1240. In 1321 it was enlarged by Blessed Andrea Gallerani, completed as it is at present in 1767 but recently restored. The facade is simple, decorated with a coping.

INSIDE: this Church has a single barrel-vaulted nave, apse and walls with stucco decorations. It is well lighted and the style is Baroque. On the right wall, behind a grating is a triptych with gilt wooden doors and ivory statues representing *the Madonna and Holy Child and Saints* (a very precious work of the 14th. century) a little graffito *Crucifix* of the 15th. century; a panel representing *Blessed Andrea Gallerani* by a disciple of Taddeo di Bartolo's probably in the 15th. century. Over the altar is the *Assumption of the Madonna*, by Lorenzo Feliciati in 1776 and a panel representing *St. Peter*, by a disciple of Lippo Memmi in the 14th. century. Over the high altar : the *Nativity of the Madonna*, by Giuseppe Nasini. On the left wall : *St. Peter*, by a disciple of Lippo Memmi's ; over the altar, *St. Paul at the Areopagus*, a very fine composition by Alessio Calvi ; *San Pellegrino*, by some unknown author. On the vaults are frescoes by Giuliano Traballesi representing *Stories about the Virgin*. In the niches are 18th. century statues some of which due to Giuseppe Mazzuoli.

Now walk up the steep Costa dell'Incrociata as far as Piazza Salimbeni (see page 134), turn to the left into Via dei Montanini at the beginning of which are two remnants of old towers with a fragment of a Roman inscription : *Vero et Vale* (referring to names of Consuls).

Fig. 63 - Santa Maria delle nevi - Matteo di Giovanni: *The Madonna of the Snow* (a detail).

Fig. 64 - Antiporto di Camollia with the column that commemorates the encounter of Eleonor of Portugal and Fredrick III.

Soon after is the quaint little facade of the ORATORY OF ST. MARY OF THE SNOW (Oratorio di Santa Maria delle Nevi), built in 1470-1471 by order of Giovanni Cinughi the Bishop of Pienza and Montalcino, to the design of Francesco di Giorgio Martini. It has a polygonal apse, a pretty Renaissance facade and bell housing, all made of brick.

INSIDE there is a single nave on two arches. To be admired is the lovely altar screen by Matteo di Giovanni: *the Madonna and the Holy Child, Angels and St. Peter, St. Jerome, St. Lawrence and St. Catherine.* This picture is generally called the *Madonna della Neve* and was painted in 1477 (Fig. 63). Apart from the high artistic value of the whole composition, here the Master succeeded in representing in an exceptional happy way the spontaneous charm of the little Child (remark the pretty little arm strechted out with childish curiosity to touch the bowl full of snow that a Saint is offering the Madonna). On the steps of the screen are three stories, with figures of Saints inserted between them, illustrating scenes from the legend of the origin of the Basilica of Santa Maria Maggiore in Rome. The first of these stories represents the snow storm that marked out the foundations of the Basilica; the second shows Pope Liberius starting the construction of the Basilica; the third shows the same Pope Liberius consecrating the Church.

Further down, on the right hand side of the same street is the CHURCH OF ST. ANDREW (Chiesa di Sant'Andrea). This building was at first in pure Romanesque style but it was all rebuilt except the apse in the 18th. century. Inside there is a single nave and cruciform vaults. Over the altar is a triptych by Giovanni di Paolo representing the *Coronation of the Virgin with St. Peter and St. Andrew,* painted in 1445; over the right altar is the *Madonna and Child with St. Anne* ascribed to Martino di Bartolomeo (found in 1959); over the left altar some fragments of 14th. c. frescoes. The next corner on the right is that of Via Garibaldi. Walk down this road as far as no. 28 on the right where, below the level of the street behind a gate, is the CHURCH OF THE COMPANY OF ST. SEBASTIAN (Chiesa della Compagnia di San Sebastiano). This building dates back to the 15th. century but the narthex is even older; it was restored in the 17th. century. Inside are several frescoes of the Life of St. Sebastian, by Pietro Sorri, Cristoforo Casolani and Rutilio Manetti. Over the altar is the wooden *Crucifix* which is said to have been given to the Compagnia della Morte (Death Company) by St. Bernardine. In the Chapels are a fine *Madonna* by Francesco Rustici, a copy of the Company's Standard painted by Sodoma in 1525 (in 1786 the original was sent to the Uffizi Gallery in Florence) and four bier heads by Girolamo del Pacchia.

[Just passed the nearby English Church of St. Peter is a house called the CASA DELLA CONSUMA where the famous « *Brigata Spendereccia* » (the Spendthrift Brigade) wasted 200.000 florins in twenty months (this is mentioned by Dante in his *Inferno,* XXIX, vv. 125-152). Then comes the Barriera di San Lorenzo and Viale Mazzini which leads to the railway station].

Now the visitor should go back to the beginning of Via Garibaldi and turn to the right into Via Camollia. In this street is PALAZZO CHIGI BENEDETTI of the 14th. century, PALAZZO BRANCADORI E PALAZZO PIERI in front of which is the CHURCH OF ST. BARTHOLOMEW (Chiesa di San Bartolomeo) once called of Santi Anastasio and Vincenzo, a 13th. century building with an old belfry and, on the outside wall a fresco of the *Redeemer.* In this Church is buried Pinturicchio. There is a delightful *Madonna and Child,* by Vecchietta, the *Madonna with Angels* by some disciple of the school of Sano di Pietro and a *banner* with the figures of Sant'Anastasio and San Vincenzo painted by Bernardino Fungai.

At the ARCO DI FONTEGIUSTA (the arch of Fontegiusta) turn to the left into Via di Fontegiusta where is

THE CHURCH OF FONTEGIUSTA
(Chiesa di Fontegiusta)

the brick facade is decorated with a single gable and a rose-window; this fine Renaissance building is the work of Francesco di Cristoforo Fedeli and Giacomo di Giovanni da Como in 1482-84. Over the marble portal sculptured by Urbano da Cortona in 1489 is a bas-relief representing the *Madonna and Holy Child with Angels.* The side walls have ogival windows. Into this Church the exultant

Fig. 65 - The Church of Fontegiusta - Inside view.

Fig. 66 - Fontegiusta - B. Peruzzi: *The Sibyl* (detail).

people of Siena carried the tropheys of victory conquered at the battle of Poggio Imperiale against the Florentines in 1479.

THE INSIDE of this fine Church is square with four pillars and composite capitals (fig. 65); the vaults are cruciform, ribbed and richly decorated (apply to the door keeper in the court-yard on the right side of the Church).

The entrance wall: the stained glass screen made to Guidoccio Cozzarelli's design in the 15th. century represents the *Madonna and Holy Child with St. Catherine and St. Bernardine*. Placed all around are old weapons and the shoulder blade of a cetacean which are supposed to have been offered to the Madonna di Fontegiusta by Chrisopher Columbus on his return from America. According to tradition, in fact, he studied at Siena and met his first lady love in Camollia. Over the altar is a fresco of the *Visitation*, by Michelangelo Anselmi; beneath it are two small 14th. century panels with the heads of Apostles. In the corner is a 15th. century bronze ciborium ascribed to Lorenzo Marrina. Right wall, first altar: *Jesus, Mary and two Saints* ascribed to Francesco Vanni; below is a painted wooden statue of *St. Bernardine*. Second altar: the *Coro-*

— 172 —

nation of Mary and four Saints, by Bernardino Fungai. High up at the end of the wall is a very elegant chantry.

The High Altar is an amazing marble work of the Renaissance period produced by Lorenzo Marrina with the collaboration of Michele Cioli da Settignano in 1509-1519. The « *Pietà* » in the lunette is also due to the same Cioli (1517) but the fresco of the *Madonna and Holy Child* is by some unknown Master of the 14th. century; this painting is generally covered.

In the lunette on the wall of the high altar is a fresco representing *the Assumption*, by Girolamo di Benvenuto in 1515; on the sides are some spoilt frescoes by Ventura Salimbeni. On the left wall, over the central door is *Christ carrying the Cross* ascribed to Sodoma; against the wall is a little bronze holy water stoup due to Giovanni delle Bombarde (1430). Over the altar is a *Sybil annuncing the birth of the Redeemer to Augustus* (fig. 66), a celebrated fresco by Baldassare Peruzzi about the year 1528. In the corner a painted wooden statue of the 15th. century representing *St. Sebastian*. On the entrance wall is a panel by Riccio representing *the Plague in Siena in* 1348.

Now go back to Via Camollia and turn to the left. Not far off is the CHURCH OF ST. PETER « alla Magione » (Chiesa di San Pietro alla Magione), once of the Templars, then of the Knights of the Order of Malta. It has a single gable, a Gothic portal and little pendant arches recently restored, a single nave and an adjoining Renaissance Chapel. HOUSE no. 176 belonged TO BALDASSARRE PERUZZI (see the epigraph). The visitor is, now, near PORTA CAMOLLIA, a 14th. century building restored by Alessandro Casolani in 1604. On the outside is the welcoming inscription: *Cor magis tibi Sena pandit* (Rather than her doors Siena opens her heart to the visitor).

Beyond Porta Camollia is the broad modern Viale Vittorio Emanuele II. On the left, before reaching the ANTIPORTO which was an advanced defensive fortress built in the 14th. century, among green flower beds stands a column bearing the coats-of-arms of the Holy Roman Empire and those of Portugal to commemorate the encounter of Emperor Fredrick III of Austria with Eleonora of Portugal, his betrothed, on Febraury 24th. 1452 (fig. 64). This meeting was arranged by Enea Silvio Piccolomini, at that time Bishop of Siena, later on Pope

Pius II (see the fresco by Pinturicchio inside the Piccolomini Library in the Cathedral, page 85).

[About 1 km. outside the Antiporto is PALAZZO DEI DIAVOLI otherwise Turchi, now called Buonsignori, a mediaeval brick building enlarged and decorated in 1460 by Antonio Federighi. It has a cylindrical tower and a simple but elegant chapel where is treasured a terracotta ascribed to Federighi representing the *Assumption*].

Walk back to town through Via Camollia and at the cross road turn to the right into Via dei Gazzani. On the left hand side of this street is the CHURCH OF ST. STEPHEN'S (di Santo Stefano), a 12th. century building restored in 1641, and again by Agenore Socini in 1903. The facade is simple with a single gable and decorative brick structures. It has a single nave. Over the right altar is the *Visitation*, by Rutilio Manetti. Over the High Altar is a many-panelled picture with the *Madonna and Child* in the middle, the figures of *Saints* at the sides, and up above the *Annunciation*, by Andrea Vanni in 1400; the foot steps are decorated with the *Crucifixion* and *Stories of St. Stephen* by Giovanni di Paolo.

By now the visitor has reached the LIZZA, the spacious and pleasant pubblic gardens made in 1779 to Antonio Matteucci's design and enlarged in 1872 according to Pietro Marchetti's plan. Here is the monument to Giuseppe Garibaldi with Raffaello Romanelli's reliefs (1896). The garden reaches on the right as far as the FORTEZZA DI SANTA BARBARA (the fortress of Santa Barbara) built by Cosimo I dei Medici to the design of Baldassare Lanci di Urbino in 1560. Admirable is the view of the town.

In the basement of the left wing of the Fortress - where, at the time of the fall of the old Sienese Republic, the Florentines established their headquarters - is now the permanent exhibition of Italian wines called ENOTECA ITALICA PERMANENTE for the sale of typical Italian wines.

When leaving the Fortress walk to Piazza Antonio Gramsci and then through via Malavolti to Piazza Matteotti. From this square through Via Pianigiani, Via Salimbeni and Via Banchi di Sopra go back to Piazza del Campo.

The Surroundings

THE PROVINCE OF SIENA

Many are the places full of historical and artistic interest in the Sienese province; in fact, every little country town or village has precious treasures of art worth seeing.

Quite near Siena, within an hour's trip or so, are : the BASILICA and CONVENT OF SAN BERNARDINO ALL'OSSERVANZA, the hermitages of LECCETO and SAN LEONARDO AL LAGO, the CASTLE OF THE « QUATTRO TORRI » (the four towers), the castle of BELCARO, the CERTOSA OF MAGGIANO and that OF PONTIGNANO, the villas of MONASTERO, SANTA COLOMBA, CETINALE, VICOBELLO, TORRE FIORENTINA; the hill of MONTEAPERTI where on September 4th., 1260 was fought the battle between the Sienese and the Florentines, mentioned by Dante Alighieri; the PIEVASCIATA.

A little farther away from Siena, even for a short stay are :

On the way to Florence, from Porta Camollia (see page 173) MONTERIGGIONI mentioned by Dante in the XXXI canto of his « *Inferno* »; STAGGIA with the remnants of the old Rocca (fortress) built in 1432; POGGIBONSI with, very near, the Fortress of Poggio Imperiale built by Giuliano da Sangallo, and the 14th. century BASILICA OF SAN LUCCHESE; COLLE DI VAL D'ELSA, the birth place of Arnolfo di Cambio; SAN GIMIGNANO, the town called « la città delle belle torri » (the town of the beautiful towers); BROLIO IN CHIANTI, famous for the exquisite wine and, very near, in the same region Castellina, Radda and Gaiole.

On the way to Rome, outside Porta Romana (see page 150) are ; BUONCONVENTO, where Harry VII of Luxemburg died in the year 1313; MONTEOLIVETO MAGGIORE, the famous Benedictine Monastery; MONTALCINO, the last stronghold of Sienese freedom with, nearby, the ABBAZIA DI SANT'ANTIMO which dates back to Charlemagne; SAN GIOVANNI D'ASSO and TREQUANDA; SAN QUIRICO D'ORCIA with its beautiful romanesque Collegiata (Parish Church) and near by the thermae of BAGNO VIGNONI and those of BAGNI SAN FILIPPO; CASTI-

GLIONE D'ORCIA (connected with the life of St. Catherine); PIENZA the town of the purest Italian renaissance; MONTE-PULCIANO the birth place of Poliziano; CHIANCIANO TERME with the celebrated thermae; CHIUSI with the Etruscan Museum and tombs; SARTEANO with its typical Sienese « Rocca » (stronghold), of the 13th. century; CETONA the birth place of Luca Contile, the poet; SAN CASCIANO DEI BAGNI with its famous water; RADICOFANI called the eagle's nest; at the foot of Mount Amiata ABBADIA SAN SALVATORE rich in mercury; PIANCASTAGNAIO with the remains of the stronghold of the Aldobrandeschi, in the midst of splendid chestnut woods.

On the way to Arezzo, outside Porta Pispini (see page 153) are : ASCIANO with its Museum of sacred art; CASTELNUOVO BERARDENGA, RAPOLANO TERME, SINALUNGA and TORRITA DI SIENA.

On the way to Grosseto, outside Porta San Marco (see page 130) are : BADIA DI PONTE ALLO SPINO; ROSIA with the nearby ABBAZIA VALLOMBROSANA DI SANTA MUSTIOLA a TORRI, of the 11th. century; the ABBEY OF SAN GALGANO the grandiose ruins of which are important for a complete study of the Tuscan Gothic architecture; MONTICIANO and CHIUSDINO.

Here is some information on the best monuments and famous places :

The BASILICA DELL'OSSERVANZA. - Outside Porta Ovile at about two kilometers and a half from the town (see page 140) either from Porta Camollia (see page 173) or from the Barriera di San Lorenzo (see page 170), on a hill called Colle della Capriola from where a delightful view of Siena can be enjoyed. It was founded by Bernardino Albizzeschi (St. Bernardine of Siena) on the site of an old hermitage of the 13th. century. The Church was restored in 1949 after damage through aerial bombardment in 1944 (fig. 67). It is partially ascribed to Francesco di Giorgio Martini.

The Church has a single nave with eight open Chapels, a presbitery and a dome. Worthy of attention are two statues of the *Annunciation* and the glazed terracotta altarpiece produced by Andrea della Robbia representing *the Coronation of the Virgin,* a terracotta representing « Pietà » by Giovanni di Paolo in the 16th. century, a *Madonna and Saints* by Maestro dell'Osservanza a reliquary for *St. Bernardine's gown,* by Francesco di Antonio in 1454, *St. Bernardine's portrait* by Pietro di Giovanni in 1439. In the Convent is *St. Bernardine's Cell,* lately rebuilt, with some of

QVESTA · E · LENTRATA · ELVSCITA · diChECho · diChECho
CINVChi · ChAMARLENCho · diCABELLA · PVNO · AÑO · CON
INCIAдo · Adi · PRIMO · diGENAIO · MCCCCLXXII · EFINEдo · Ad
VLTIMO · didICENbRE · MCCCCLXXIII · E dVGO · bVONAGIONTA ·
QVESTI · SONO · IPRIMI · ASICh CRITORE · EdIPIERO · dALDOBRAN
VITORI · MEO · diTOTO · CEERETANI · E IACOMO · diGALGAN
NICOlo · dIMS bARTALOMEO bIChI · E · diFRANCIESCho · diS
diMATIO · dANTONIO · dINRI CARO · EdITOMAXO · di
dANGOLO · MALAVOITI MAVRITIO · LVTI · E · di8
E · diSARdVINO · NOTAIO dOMENICO · diXFANO · N

SANO DI PIETRO (Siena, 1406-1481)

*Le nozze di Lucrezia Malavolti col conte Roberto di Sanse-
verino* (Tavoletta di Gabella - Archivio di Stato)

*Les noces de Lucrezia Malavolti avec le Comte Roberto de
Sanseverino* (Petit retable de Gabella - Archives de l'Etat)

*Wedding of Lucrezia Malavolti with Count Roberto di San-
severino* (State Archives)

*Hochzeit der Lucrezia Malavolti mit dem Grafen Roberto
di Sanseverino* (Staatsarchiv)

VIII.

Fig. 67 - The Basilica dell'Osservanza.

the Saint's remembrances and a terracotta ascribed to Urbano da Cortona. In the adjoining Museum are treasured chorals, jewellery, and a precious wooden sculpture representing the *Mutilated Head of Christ* carved by Lando di Pietro in 1337.

CERTOSA DI PONTIGNANO - At 8 km. from Porta Ovile (see page 140). It was founded by Bindo Petroni in 1343 and supressed in 1810. Soon after, however, it was partially turned into a villa. In 1959 the Government purchased it to found a « Seminario universitario » (University seminary) (1961) to honour the name of Mario Bracci the Sienese « Giudice Costituzionale ».

There are three CLOISTERS. One is in the Renaissance style, with a well-head and a fine 15th. century portal

Fig. 68 - Siena (surroundings) - Certosa di Pontignano - One of the cloisters.

(fig. 68); the smaller one has a brick loggia an a 14th. century portal; the third is larger, decorated with frescoes after the style of Bernardino Poccetti. In the CHURCH, frescoes of the life of the Certosini friars by Bernardino Poccetti and Francesco Vanni and a fine 16th. century wooden chancel. In the adjoining « CAPPELLONE » (big Chapel) there is a good *Crucifixion* by Francesco Vanni, and some paintings by Giuseppe Nasini and his pupils.

BELCARO at 5 km. from Porta Fontebranda (see p. 154) and at about the same distance from Porta San Marco (see page 130).

Fig. 69 - Siena (surroundings) - Belcaro - Baldassare Peruzzi: *A ceiling in the Loggia.*

The old castle built in 1199 belonged to the Turamini family who called Baldassare Peruzzi to build the palace on the side of the « rocca » (fortress), the beautiful Loggia and the Chapel. The same artist painted *Il Giudizio di Paride* (Paride's Choice) on the walls of the atrium (hall) and decorated the Loggia and the Chapel with friezes and figures (1536) (fig. 69). During the siege of Siena Gian Giacomo de' Medici, Marquis of Marignano (see page 16) established his headquarters there.

LECCETO (fig. 70) at about 5 km. from Belcaro (see above) in the midst of a wood of evergreen oaks. (326 m. above sea level). These trees are called in Italian « Lecci » from where the name of « Lecceto » was derived. It is a very old Agostinian Convent. The building as it is to be seen now dates back to the 14th. century.

In the atrium (hall) there are some good but ruined monocoloured frescoes by Paolo di Neri in 1343, ranged as

Fig. 70 - The ex-Convent of Lecceto

Fig. 71 - Siena (surroundings) - The hill of Monteaperti.

follows : *Hell, Paradise. Deeds of Mercy.* The cloister is frescoed with stories from the life of St. Augostine. These ruined pantings date back to the 14th. century.

SAN LEONARDO AL LAGO - This 12th. century Agostinian Convent at three kilometres and a half from Belcaro (see above) is the hermitage where Blessed Agostino Novello died in 1309. He was a knight at the Court of King Manfredi. Now he is buried in the Basilica of Sant'Agostino in Siena (see page 125) and the old Convent has been abandoned.

In the CHURCH there is a good frescoe by Lippo Vanni and some spoilt 14th. century paintings of the Sienese school. In the REFECTORY there are some spoilt frescoes by Giovanni di Paolo.

MONTEAPERTI - Is the name of the hill where the Sienese defeated the Florentines on April 2nd., 1260. It is situated in the Arbia valley between Biena and Malena, at about one kilometre and a half from Porta Pispini, Siena (see page 153). On the top of the hill, surrounded with cypresses, stands a commemorative pyramid. The battle was described by Dante in the XXXII Canto of his *Inferno* (fig. 71).

CASTELLINA IN CHIANTI

CASTELLINA IN CHIANTI - This pleasant little place at 20 km. from Porta Camollia (see page 173) is 288 m. above sea level and enjoys the view of three valleys: the Arbia Valley, the Elsa valley and the Pesa valley. It is a quaint village surrounded with medieval walls and protected by a huge battlemented fortress and tower. In the neighbourhood are the castles of Recine, Meleto, Castagnoli, Lecchi, Cacchiano, Spaltenna and Vertine.

In the PARISH CHURCH there is a detached fresco of the *Madonna delle Grazie* by Lorenzo di Bicci.
Outside the village gates are four paleo-Etruscan hypogea.

RADDA IN CHIANTI

RADDA IN CHIANTI - On the side of a hill at 12 km. from Castellina (see above) in a panoramic position 533 m. above sea level. The old walls and towers are still admirable.

In the PALAZZO COMUNALE (Town hall) there are some coats of-arms of the « Podestà » (bailiffs), a good 15th. century fresco of the Sienese school and an autograph of Francesco Ferrucci's who was « Podestà » in 1527.

MONTERIGGIONI

MONTERIGGIONI - At 13½ km. outside Porta Camollia (see page 173) in a panoramic position 274 m. above sea level. It was built as a castle-fortress to defend Siena in 1213, and surrounded with a circular wall 570 m. long with fourteen square towers originally much higher than at present (fig. 72). Dante mentioned it in the XXXI Canto of his « *Inferno* ».

BADIA A ISOLA

BADIA A ISOLA - At 3 km. from Monteriggioni (see above) 200 m. above s. l. It is an old Cistercian Abbey called San Salvatore and San Cirino but it got its name of « a Isola » (the island) from the bogs which in olden times lay all around it. The Romanesque Church dates back to the year 1000. The three aisles, the three apses and the baptismal font show Gothic traditions; they date back to 1419.

See the frescoes by Vecchietta and Vincenzo Tamagni, the well known *Madonna* by « Maestro di Badia a Isola » (by some ascribed to Duccio di Buoninsegna when young), a panel by Sano di Pietro and a roman cinerary urn containing the bones of San Cirino (1198).

POGGIBONSI - At 13 1/2 km. from Monteriggioni (see above3 along the railroad from Siena to Empoli (115 m. above s. l.). It is the industrial and commercial centre of all the Chianti region. There are some old Gothic palaces and the Palazzo Pretorio with a battlemented tower, built where once stood the little village of Marturi.

In the 14th. century CHURCH OF SAN LORENZO E SANT'AGOSTINO (partially rebuilt) see the wooden *Crucifix* ascribed to Giovanni di Agostino in 1325. In the 19th. century COLLEGIATA (Parish Church) see the baptismal font made in the year 1341.

At 1.600 m. along the road which goes from the *Fonte delle Fate* (the Fairies' Fount) to the ruins of *Poggio Bonizzo* and to the unfinished Rocca (fortress) of *Poggio Imperiale* stands the CONVENT OF SAN LUCCHESE (m. 201) the

Fig. 72 - Monteriggioni. The old walls surrounding the village.

Fig. 73 - Poggibonsi (surroundings) - The Basilica of San Lucchese.

first franciscan tertiary to enter the Franciscan Order (1221) (fig. 73). The Rocca of Poggio Imperiale was built by Giuliano da San Gallo in 1478 to Lorenzo il Magnifico's order.

In the 13th. century BASILICA is treasured the body of San Lucchese; the Chapel is decorated with paintings by Cennino Cennini, Paolo di Giovanni Fei and Bartolo di Fredi. There is also a Della Robbia dossal of the year 1514, a carved cupboard decorated with figures ascribed to Ugolino da Siena und Duccio di Buoninsegna. In the REFECTORY see the fresco by Gerino da Pistoia in 1513.

COLLE DI VAL D'ELSA - This busy little town lies at 7 1/2 km. from Poggibonsi (see above). It consits of *Colle basso o piano* (low Colle) and *Colle alto o borgo* (high Colle). Colle alto is the ancient part of the town within the old mediaeval walls and gates. Worthy of attention

Fig. 74 - Colle di Val d'Elsa - Arnolfo di Cambio's house.

arc.: Porta Volterrana, a 14th. century building with two cylindrical towers; the tower-house where in 1301 Arnolfo di Cambio was born, the well known architect and sculptor (fig. 75); Palazzo Campana; the house where from 1503 to 1507 Antonio Pagliari da Veroli lived, the humanistic precursor of the Reformation. He was generally known as Aonio Paleario.

COLLE BASSO - (137 m. above s.l.). In the 11th. century CHURCH OF SANT'AGOSTINO there are paintings by Taddeo di Bartolo, Lodovico Cigoli, a 15th. century wooden *Crucifix* and a marble tabernacle by Baccio da Montelupo.

COLLE ALTO (223 m. above s.l.) - In the CHURCH AND ORATORY OF ST. CATHERINE there is a fine holy water stoup of the 16th. century, a scene composed of six terracotta figures called *"Pietà"* di Cecco di Gambassi. In the CONSERVATORIO FEMMINILE there is a good 15th. century wooden statue, and two 16th. century silver reliquaries. In the Cathedral, which was built in 1603, there is a 15th. century marble pulpit, a wrought iron gate of the 15th. century, the tabernacle made for the relic known as the *Chiodo* (nail) the work either of Benedetto da Maiano or of Mino da Fiesole. a bronze lectern by Pietro Tacca, a bronze Crucifix ascribed to Giamoblogna in 1268, the baptismal font made in 1465, miniated chorals of the 15th. and 16th. centuries, a 12th. century communion - cup and a 16th. century pyx. In the ARCHBISHOPIC there are some frescoes of the school of the Lorenzetti brothers representing hunts and the deeds of the Crusaders. In the MUSEUM see the pictures by Rutilio Manetti, Sebastiano Conca, and Pier Francesco Fiorentino. In the CHURCH OF SANTA MARIA CANONICA there is a tabernacle by Benozzo Gozzoli.

SAN GIMIGNANO is 37 km. outside Porta Camollia (see page 173) and 12 km. from Poggibonsi (see above) on top of a hill 390 metres above sea level overlooking the Elsa valley. There is a very fine old castle which was enlarged during the 10th. century. This town lived as a wealthy free Commune through the 13th. and 14th. centuries but after much struggling it fell under the Florentine domination in 1353. History has left marks on the arstistic monuments of this town which show Pisan, Sienese and Florentine influences. San Gimignano is known as the « Città dalle belle torri » (the town of the beautiful towers) and appears like a delightful mediaeval panel painted with an architectonic scenery nowhere else to be found (fig. 75).

Fig. 75 - San Gimignano - A view of the towers.

PIAZZA DELLA CISTERNA is triangular with a fine well-head in the middle; from here many of the severe buildings and massive towers can be admired. The COLLEGIATA (the Collegiate Church) has a 13th. century facade restored in later ages; the inside is Romanesque with a nave and two aisles covered with 14th. century vaults. The once smaller transept was enlarged by Giuliano da Maiano in 1466-68. On the wall near the entrance are frescoes representing the *Martyrdom of St. Sebastian*, by Benozzo Gozzoli (1465) and *the Last judgement*, by Taddeo di Bartolo (1395). In the right aisle: *Scenes from the life of Jesus*, by Barna (about the year 1380) finished off later on by Giovanni d'Asciano, Barna's nephew (fig. 76). In the Chapel of Santa Fina: relics of this fifteen year old Saint of San Gimignano are on Benedetto da Maiano's altar (1468): on the walls frescoes representing the *Saint's Death and Funeral* by Domenico Ghirlandaio in 1468; the vault was frescoed by Sebastiano Mainardi. Left aisle: *scenes from the old Testament*, by Bartolo di Fredi in 1356. In St. John's Oratory: Domenico Ghirlandaio's *Annunciation*. *T*he Chancel has fine stalls carved in 1490 and frescoes painted by Pollaiolo (1483) and Benozzo Gozzoli (1466).

Fig. 76 - San Gimignano - The Parish Church - Barna and Giovanni
d'Asciano: *The Crucifixion.*

The PALAZZO DEL POPOLO or DEL PODESTÀ designed by Arnolfo di Cambio in 1283 has a tower called the Torre Grossa
(the big tower) which dates back to 1300. In the Council
Hall where Dante Alighieri spoke in favour of the Guelph
League on May 8th. 1300 is a large *Maestà* by Lippo Memmi (1317) imitating the same scene painted by Simone Martini his brother-in-law in the Town Hall of Siena (see

page 44), and friezes representing *hunting scenes and battles* (1292). The Museum which has only recently been arranged contains works by Filippino Lippi, Pinturicchio, Taddeo di Bartolo, Bartolo di Fredi, Niccolò di Ser Sozzo Tegliacci and Coppo di Marcovaldo. In another room are some precious potteries. The room of the Podestà inside the tower is decorated with *Love Scenes* ascribed to Memmo di Filippuccio (14th. century).

The CHIESA DI SANT'AGOSTINO (the Church of St. Augustine) is a 13th. century Gothic building with a single nave. In the Chapel of San Bartolo, the protector of the town who died in 1494, are frescoes by Bastiano Mainardi in 1500. In the chancel is a cycle of frescoes illustrating the *Life of St. Augustine,* by Benozzo Gozzoli in 1464-65, all most important from the stylistic point of view. From the ROCCA (fortress) high up above the town a splendid panorama may be enjoyed.

At about 3 km., almost hidden among rows of cypresses stands the beautiful PIEVE DI SANTA MARIA DI CELLOLE, a 13th. century building with three naves resting on huge pillars with finely sculptured capitals. Here Giacomo Puccini drew inspiration for the scenery and the music of his « *Suor Angelica* ».

BUONCONVENTO, the place where Harry VII of Luxemburg, the Emperor mentioned by Dante as the peacemaker in Italy, died on August 24th. 1313. It is situated at 27 km. from Porta Romana, Siena (see page 150) within its mediaeval walls.

In the 16th. century PARISH CHURCH - restored in 1705 - there are some paintings by Giovanni Pacchiarotti, Sano di Pietro and Matteo di Giovanni. In the adjoining MUSEUM see the pictures by Segna di Bonaventura, Andrea di Bartolo, Pietro di Domenico, Guidoccio Cozzarelli, Girolamo di Benvenuto and Girolamo del Pacchia, fine jewellery of the 15th. and 17th. centuries some bier-heads of the 16th. and 18th. centuries.

MONTEOLIVETO MAGGIORE is 36 km. outside Porta Romana (see page 150) on the left just after Buonconvento. It is a celebrated Benedictine Abbey and the Mother House of the Olivetan Monks (fig. 79) founded and dedicated to Santa Scolastica in 1313 when the Sienese Bernardo Tolomei (and two other nobles called Patrizio Patrizi and Ambrogio Piccolomini), retired to live a

Fig. 77 - Monteoliveto Maggiore - Sodoma (Giov. Ant. Bazzi): *Self portrait* (a detail).

Fig. 78 - Monteoliveto Maggiore - Luca Signorelli: *A woman
serving a monk* (a detail).

hermit's life in that place which was then called the
« desert or Accona ». Based on the rule of St. Benedict,
in 1319 it became the Congregation of Santa Maria di
Monteoliveto, a rule which has contributed much to the
fields of science and art and is considered as one of the
greatest Monasteries in Italy. In 1954 an *Institute of
pathology of books* was founded there, a very interesting
scientific activity.

The architecture of the building as well as the pretty
country-side are most suggestive. The building looks like
a turreted castle with a battlemented tower at the entrance
with two Della Robbia terracottas one representing the
Madonna and the other *St. Benedict.* In the delightful park
are many Chapels; behind the altar in St. Benedict's Chapel (rebuilt in the year 1760) lie the remains of the founder.
The Gothic Church was built from 1400 to 1417 and restored
inside soon after the year 1772. It has the shape of a Latin
cross with a single nave. In the Chancel are some splendid
carved stalls due to Giovanni da Verona in 1503-05 and a

fine lectern by Raffaello da Brescia in 1518. In the SA-CRISTY are some nice 15th. century wooden benches. On the walls of the main Cloister (15th. century) is an admirable cycle of frescoes illustrating thirty-six scenes from the *Life of San Benedetto da Norcia;* nine scenes are due to the masterhand of Luca Signorelli (1497-1498; see fig. 78) and the rest to Giovanni Antonio Bazzi called Sodoma (1505-1508; see fig. 77). The REFECTORY contains some 17th. century frescoes. The LIBRARY has three naves and a very elegant vestible designed by Frate Giovanni da Verona in 1518; this same friar carved the entrance door and the cupboard and sculptured one of the candelabra. Here are treasured some miniatel chorals of the 15th. century and some very precious ceramics.

MONTALCINO lies 45 km. outside Porta Romana (see p. 150) and 13 km. from Buonconvento (see above) in a very good position at 564 metres above sea level; it en-

Fig. 79 - Asciano (surroundings). Archicenobio di Monteoliveto Maggiore - The Church.

Fig. 80 - Montalcino (surroundings) - The Church of Sant'Antimo.

Fig. 81 - Montalcino - The Sienese Fortress.

joys splendid views of the valleys of the rivers Ombrone, Asso and Orcia. In 814 it was already known as a feud of the nearby Abbey of Sant'Antimo; after much struggling between the Sienese and the Florentines it passed to the former who built the fortress (1361). Montalcino proved faithful to Siena; during the siege the Sienese exiles were welcome there and found support in their attempt to reestablish the defeated Republic (1555-57) (see page 17).

In the ROCCA (the fortress: fig.81) is still to be seen the *standard* painted by Sodoma for the last defenders of the Sienese Republic. Inside the Palazzo Comunale (the Town Hall), a brick and stone building with a fine tower belonging to the 13th. and 14th. centuries, are ranged the rooms of the Museum with a very good collection of pictures dating from the 14th. century to the 16th., some majolicas of the 14th. century and two celebrated miniated Bibles one of which is of the 12th. century. In the Seminary adjoining the Chiesa di Sant'Agostino (the Church of St. Augustine) there is an interesting MUSEUM OF SACRED ART with paintings by Bartolo di Fredi, Girolamo di Benvenuto and Segna di Bonaventura and, besides, an important group of polychromic wooden statues by Sienese artists of the 14th. and 15th. centuries.

SANT'ANTIMO. At about 10 km. from Montalcino (see above), is the loveliest Romanesque Church in Sienese territory (318 m. above s.l.). At first it belonged to the Benedictine Monks, then to the Guglielmiti (1291). It was built at the time of Charlemagne whose son Ludovico il Pio endowed in with a large number of Churches in Tuscany (from the 10th. to the 12th. century). It was suppressed in 1492.

The CHURCH is very interesting. Started in 1118 after the Romanesque-Lombard style, with some foreign influences, the nave and lateral aisles have huge pointed arches resting upon columns decorated with delightful capitals; over these runs a travertine and alabaster gallery with fine windows (fig. 80). The tribune of the high altar is surrounded with a semi-circle of pillars. Below is the crypt, also rounded with one nave and lateral aisles (9th. century). In the apse are the remains of frescoes ascribed to Spinello Aretino. Just inside the entrance door is a 13th. century wooden *Crucifix*. A flight of steps leads to the right tribune where are ranged five rooms with floreal decorations now hardly visible (15th. century).

Fig. 82 - San Quirico d'Orcia - One of the Parish Church portals.

SAN GIOVANNI D'ASSO - At 10 km. from Torrenieri before turning towards Montalcino (see above). On the highest spot of the village (310 m. above s.l.) stands the old 12th. century castle with its elegant gothic windows Inside there is a delightful mantle-piece and a 15th. century. wash-stand.

Nearby is the CHURCH OF SAN PIETRO IN VILLORE, a 12th. century building with a crypt and three aisles.

TREQUANDA is at 10 km. from San Giovanni d'Asso (see above). It is a characteristic little village 462 m. above sea level, gathered around a huge 13th. century castle with a cylindrical battlemented tower.

In the PARISH CHURCH see Giovanni di Paolo's triptych, Sodoma's and Bartolomeo Miranda's frescoes and the carved wooden urn containing the ashes of Blessed Bonizella Piccolomini-Cacciaconti (1235-1300). This Church was built in the 11th. century.

SAN QUIRICO D'ORCIA - At 44 km. from Porta Romana (see page 150) 409, m. above sea level. It was once called San Quirico in Osenna. It is an 8th. century village on the hills that separate the Orcia Valley from the Asso Valley. Most interesting are the old walls and gates, particularly the gate called Porta dei Cappuccini with its polygonal tower.

The gothic-romanesque COLLEGIATE CHURCH is a 12th.-13th. century building with three richly decorated portals (fig. 82). Inside see the fine triptych by Sano di Pietro, the 15th. century chancel carved by Antonio Barili, once in St. John's Chapel in the Cathedral of Siena, and Count Enrico di Nassau's tomb stone; he died at San Quirico in 1451. In the CHURCH OF THE MISERICORDIA there is a fine panel of the school of Sodoma. In the CHURCH OF SANTA MARIA DI VITALETA is a fine Della Robbia terracotta and some polychrome wooden statues of the 15th. century.

BAGNO VIGNONI - At 4 km. from San Quirico d'Orcia (see above) and 306 m. above s.l. Recommended thermo-mineral baths (temperature of the wather, 52°) and mud baths for the treatment of rheumatism, arthritis, neuralgia and neuritis. St. Catherin of Siena and Lorenzo il Magnifico enjoyed the benefits of these baths.

CASTIGLIONE D'ORCIA - At 9 km. from Bagno Vignoni (see above) in a panoramic position 574 m. above s.l. Worth seeing is the fort called « Rocca degli Aldo-brandeschi ».

In the PARISH CHURCH there is a panel by Pietro Loren-zetti, and some frescoes of the Sienese school. In the CHURCH OF SANTA MARIA MADDALENA see the Madonna ascribed to Lip-po Memmi and the one painted by Vecchietta.

At 1 km. from Castiglioni there is the little mediaeval vil-lage of ROCCA D'ORCIA, otherwise Rocca a Tentennano; it is just near « Rocca Salimbeni » where St. Catherine miracu-lously learnt to write.

In the CHURCH OF SAN SIMEONE see the frescoes by Bar-tolo di Fredi and the Madonna by Giovanni di Paolo.

BAGNI SAN FILIPPO is the name of a little thermal village 21 km. from San Quirico d'Orcia (see above). It lies on the sides of Mount Amiata 500 m. above s.l. The temperature of the water varies from 25° to 52° and, according to an old legend, it seems to have sprung up

Fig. 83 Pienza - Palazzo Piccolomini - Pope Pius II's bed-room.

Fig. 84 - Pienza - Palazzo Piccolomini.

Fig. 85 - Montepulciano
The Town Hall.

from the ground where San Filippo Bonizzi touched it with stick. Recommended for the treatment of skin disease, rheumatism, arthritis, uricemia and bronchial asthma. There is also an olympic swimming pool.

PIENZA is at 53 km. from Porta Romana (see p. 150) and 12 km. from San Quirico d'Orcia (see above). This lovely little town lies on top of a hill 490 metres above sea level; it is a jewel of art originated from the transformation of the old Castle of Corsignano for the pleasure of Enea Silvio Piccolomini, later on Pope Pius II, who was born there. It was built by Bernardo Rossellino (1459-62).

In the central Piazza stands the CATHEDRAL ; it has a single nave and lateral aisles and a travertine facade which is a most splendid specimen of the architecture of the transition period from the Gothic to the Renaissance. It contains the following masterpieces : the *Assumption*, Vecchietta's masterpiece (1461) ; a *Madonna* by Sano di Pietro and another by Matteo di Giovanni in 1462 ; a delightful baptismal font by Rossellino. PALAZZO PICCOLOMINI (fig. 84) resembles somewhat Palazzo Rucellai in Florence. Next to it is a beautiful well-head built by Rossellino. The courtyard has fine

— 197 —

composite coulumns on which rests the internal facade
with three loggias all around, one above the other and a
roof-garden from where a very pretty view can be admired.
Inside the Palace in the somptuous *Hall of Arms* is
Pius II's *collection of medals* and *his bed room* (fig. 83).
THE BISHOP'S PALACE with cruciform windows is also very
fine. The ancient CASA DEI CANONICI (the house of the Canons) is now the seat of the Museum where are treasured
precious 15th. century Flemish tapestries, miniated chorals,
lovely panels painted by Sassetta, Matteo di Giovanni,
Vecchietta, Sano di Pietro, Bartolo di Fredi and Giovanni
di Paolo, Pope Pius II's vestment on which are embroidered
in coloured silks and gold no less than 150 figures; this masterpiece of embroidery was produced in England in the
14th. century.

MONTEPULCIANO - lies at 605 metres above sea level
on top of a rocky tufaceous hill 68 km. from porta Romana (see p. 150) and 14 km. from Pienza (see above); it enjoys a fine view of the Chiana Valley, of Lake Trasimeno
and of Mount Amiata. It was the birth place of Marcello Cervini later on Pope Marcellus II, (1501-1555), of
Cardinal Roberto Bellarmino (1542-1621) and of the hu-
manist poet Agnolo de' Cini known as *Poliziano* (1454-
1494). This little town reached its splendour under the
Medici, as the rich Renaissance and 15th. century architectures stand to prove.

Along the main street, called « *il Corso* », are the best
palaces : PALAZZO AVIGNONESI and TARUGI (by Jacopo Barozzi nicknamed *Vignola*), PALAZZO PAOLINI (raised by Antonio Giamberti, called *Antonio da Sangallo il Giovane*),
PALAZZO BUCELLI (cinerary urns and Latin and Etruscan
inscriptions from the excavations are let into the walls),
PALAZZO CERVINI (by Sangallo il Giovane), PALAZZO GRUGNI
(by Vignola), POLIZIANO'S HOUSE (a 14th. century building restored in the 16th.). PALAZZO BELLARMINI (the 15th.
century building where Cardinal Roberto, the Saint, was
born) ; the LOGGE DEL MERCATO (the Market Loggia) very
likely by Vignola ; the CHIESA DI SANT'AGOSTINO (Church of
St. Augustine) a Gothic- Renaissance building due to Michelozzo Michelozzi, the CHIESA DEL GESÙ (17th. century), the
CHIESA DI SANTA MARIA DEI SERVI (the Church of St. Mary
of the Servi) 14th. century, restored by Andrea del Pozzo.
In the « Piazza Grande » - the monumental centre of the
town - are : the PALAZZO COMUNALE (15th. century) built in
the Florentine style with a fine tower (fig. 85). PALAZZO TARU-

Fig. 86 - Montepulciano (surroundings). The Church of San Biagio.

GI and PALAZZO CONTUCCI (both due to Antonio da Sangallo il Vecchio) and the CATHEDRAL (restored by Ippolito Scalza in 1594); the nave and lateral aisles are richly decorated with sculptures by Michelozzo Michelozzi and one of Taddeo di Bartolo's grandiose triptychs (1401), painted wooden statues by Francesco di Valdambrino and a Della Robbia terracotta altar screen. In the nearby Via Ricci is the MUSEO CIVICO ranged in Palazzo Bombagli otherwise called « della Corte d'Assise »; it contains some important panels and canvases of the Sienese and Florentine schools and some of Luca and Andrea della Robbia's most precious terracotte.

Just outside Porta a Prato is the CHIESA DI SANT'AGNESE (the Church of St. Agnese) a 14th. century building recently restored; the body of the Dominican Agnese Segni, patroness of the town, is resting there.

On the way back at about 1 km. on the right hand side is the CHIESA DI SAN BIAGIO (the Church of St. Biagio). It has the shape of a Greek cross with a fine cupola (fig. 86). The adjoining CANONICA (rectory) is a splendid Renaissance building due to Antonio da Sangallo il Vecchio (1519-26).

CHIANCIANO TERME - At 75 km. from Porta Romana, Siena, (see page 150) and 30 km. from San Quirico d'Orcia (see above), 549 metres above sea level. It is an international resort for the treatment of liver and bilious complaints (*Acqua Santa* spring : fig. 87), hypertension, arteriosclerosis, myocardic insufficiency and vasal spasm (*Silene* mud baths). The water of *Sant'Elena* instead is good for gastric troubles and uricemia. The therapeutical properties of these waters were recommended even by the Etruscans.

The original nucleus of the old town lies in a panoramic position at 2 kilometrs' distance. The mediaeval architecture of the old castle, now the property of Count Manenti, and the Palazzo del Podestà are interesting. In the CHURCH OF THE MISERICORDIA there is a fine fresco by Luca Signorelli. In the SALA DI ARTE ANTICA (ancient art) in the Palazzo dell'Arcipretura are to be seen : a many panelled picture by an artist known as Maestro di Chianciano, a painted Cross by Maestro di San Paolo the pupil of Duccio di Buoninsegna, a 13th. century polychrome wooden statue, a 15th. century Florentine glass screen, a panel by Lorenzo di Niccolò Gerini, jewellery and some 16th. century miniated chorals. In the COLLEGIATA (Parish Church) see Rustichino's *Presepio* (Crib) and the 14th. century *Crucifix*. This Church is an 11th. century building; remark the romanesque portal.

In the neighbourhood is the CHURCH OF SANTA MARIA DELLA ROSA a renaissance building designed by Baldassare Lanci in 1585.

CHIUSI is situated at 92 km. from porta Romana, Siena, (see p. 150) and 8 km. from Chianciano Terme (see above). It is a very old town on top of a hill covered with olive groves 373 metres above sea level. It was one of the most powerful federated towns of Etruria (once called « lucomonie » and mentioned by Virgil in his *Aeneid*).

The CATHEDRAL is worthy of attention. It was built in the 12th. century and restored in the nineteenth. It has one nave with lateral aisles. Remarkable is the *Nativity* by Bernardino Fungai and a collection of miniated chorals from the Monastery of Monteoliveto Maggiore (see page 89). The TOWN MUSEUM contains many works of the Etruscan age (fig. 88). Nearby are the ETRUSCAN TOMBS : *Tomba del Granduca* (the Grand Duke's Tomb), *Tomba della Scimmia* (the Monkey's

Fig. 87 - Chianciano Terme - Acqua
Santa Spring.

Fig. 88 - Chiusi - The
Etruscan Museum - A cine-
rary urn.

Tomb), *Tomba della Pellegrina* (the Pilgrim's Tomb) and
Tomba delle Tassinaie (the Tombe of the Tassinaie). These
tombs still show their primitive architecture and internal
decorations.

SARTEANO - At 12 km. from Chianciano Terme and 10
from Chiusi (see above) 573 metres above sea level on
Mount Cetona. Like in most of the little towns of Tuscany there is a typical old castle (15th. century) with a huge
tower and a drawbridge. At 500 metres' distance there are
the radio-active waters of BAGNO SANTO (temperature:
24°) recommended for the treatment of all kinds of nervous complaints and skin diseases. In 1955 an olympic
swimming pool was built.

In the CHURCH OF SAN FRANCESCO there is Jacopo di Mino
del Pellicciaio's altar screen. Next to the Church is the
Convent with a graceful cloister. In the CHURCH OF SAN MAR-
TINO IN FORO see the paintings by Domenico Beccafumi,
Jacopo di Mino del Pellicciaio and by some artisits of Andrea di Niccolò's school. In the renaissance CHURCH OF SAN
LORENZO there is a fine ciborium sculptured by Marrina. The
16th. century Chancel is also worthy of praise; see the
paintings by Girolamo del Pacchia.

Fig 89 - Radicofani. The ruins of the Castle.

CETONA - At 6 km. from Sarteano (see above) 384 m. above sea level. The origin of this little town is Etruscan There is a 15th. century castle and, all around the town, fragments of the old walls.

In the 13th. century PARISH CHURCH there are some frescoes of the 14 th. century.

At 2 kilometres' distance is the CHURCH OF SAN FRANCESCO with some good paintings by Sano di Pietro and Benvenuto di Giovanni; nearby is the CONVENT OF SANTA MARIA DI BELVERDE (484 m. above sea level). In the Church there are some 14th. and 15th. century frescoes, mostly of the Sienese school. Just behind the Convent there are the remains of a large troglodytic village and grottoes which date back to to the brazen age. It is said that St. Francis of Assisi used to come here to pray.

SAN CASCIANO DEI BAGNI - At 15 km. from Cetona (see above) 582 m. above sea level on Monte Cetona. The houses are grouped around a characteristic old Villa shaped like a castle.

It is a thermal resort known ever since the times of the Romans. The springs are just outside the town, at about one kilometre (525 m. above sea level). The spring called *Sorgente Ficoncella* (temperature : 39°) is recommended for baths, drinks and gynaecologic treatment; the spring called *Sorgente della Piscina* (temperature : 43°) for mud baths, liver complaints rhematism and gastric complaints.

RADICOFANI -At 17 km. from San Casciano dei Bagni (see above) and 73 km. from Porta Romana, Siena (see page 150). This little mediaeval town is 896 m. above sea level around the rock where are the remains of the 11th. century stronghold which belonged to the Monks of Abbadia San Salvatore (fig. 89). In the 13th. century it was the residence of Ghino di Tacco the adventurer who presided over all the business connections between Tuscany and Rome. From the castle the panorama is splendid.

In the PALAZZO PRETORIO see the old stone coats-of-arms. In the 13th. century CHURCH OF SAN PIETRO there is a terracotta statue and some dossals of the school of Della Robbia. In the gothic CHURCH OF SANT'AGATA a glazed terracotta dossal and an 18th. century wooden statue.

ABBADIA SAN SALVATORE - At 19 km. and a half from Radicofani (see above) and 72 km. from Porta Ro-

Fig. 90 - Asciano. A room of the Museum of Sacred Art.

mana, Siena (see page 150). It is a pretty summer and winter resort 812 m. above sea level on the south side of Monte Amiata. In winter people go there to practise winter sports. The underground is rich in mercury.

The oldest Church is the ABBEY OF SAN SALVATORE, otherwise del *Monte Amiata*. It was founded in 743 and suppressed 1782. In the 11th. century Church see the fine wooden Crucifix of the 12th. century, the carved Chancel (15th. century) and in the CRYPT, which was the original Church, the 40 pillars with sculptured capitals.

The top of Mount Amiata (1734 m.) is only 13 km. and 500 m. far from the village. It is the highest peak in Tuscany. On the way to the top there are some huts where turists and sportsmen may find alla comforts : *Rifugio Amiatino* (1276 m.), *Rifugio Generale Cantore* (1420 m.) from where a ski-lift starts and also a good track for sledges, *Rifugio Siena* (1669 m.) also provided with a ski-lift, and *Rifugio La Croce,* on the top, from where one enjoys the panorama of the whole region from the Tyrrhenian Sea to the Apennines with their highest peak : il Gran Sasso d'Italia.

PIANCASTAGNAIO - At 5 km. and 500 m. from Abbadia San Salvatore (see above) 772 m. above sea level. It is a little summer resort in a panoramic position amidst lofty chestnut woods.

See the battlemented gate of the town, the delapidated castle (rocca) of the Aldobrandeschi and the old Palazzo Bourbon del Monte. Near the village is the 13th. century CONVENT OF SAN BARTOLOMEO and the CHURCH OF THE MADONNA DI SAN PIETRO.

ASCIANO - At 25 km. from Porta Pispini, Siena (see page 153) or even from Porta Romana, Siena (see page 150). This little town lies at 200 m. above sea level. In the old palaces are treasured many admirable works of art.

In the PARISH CHURCH (*Collegiata*) OF SANT'AGATA see the frescoes ascribed to Girolamo del Pacchia and to Sodoma, and the 15th. century wooden Crucifix. In the MUSEO D'ARTE SACRA (Museum of Sacred Art) there are pieces of a very important Chancel and some good 14th. and 15th. century paintings by the following Sienese artists : Barna, Giovanni da Asciano, an anonymous pupil of Duccio di Buoninsegna's, Ambrogio Lorenzetti, Pietro di Giovanni d'Ambrogio, Maestro dell'Osservanza or Sassetta, Taddeo and Andrea di Bartolo, Matteo di Giovanni and Giovanni di Paolo. See also the polychrome statues by Francesco di Valdambrino (fig. 90). In a house in *Via del Canto* there is a very fine Roman mosaic floor. In the recent little ETRUSCAN MUSEUM (Museo Etrusco) are treasured all the objects found in the necropolis of Poggio Pinci at 5 km. from the town. On the walls of the barn of CASA CORBOLI are frescoed *the four season of the year* by an anonymous pupil of Ambrogio Lorenzetti. In the CHURCH OF SAN FRANCESCO there is a famous gothic panel by Matteo di Giovanni.

CASTELLO DI BROLIO - (The Castle of Brolio) - is a pentagonal fortress-castle on the side of a hill at 12 km. from Radda in Chianti (see above) and 23 km. from Porta Ovile, Siena (see page 140), 533 m. above sea level. It was already complete in the 19th. century, with ramparts and a ditch all around it. In 1141 it became the property of the noble Ricasoli family who had a gothic palace built within the precincts and lived in it. Bettino Ricasoli, the well known statesman died there in 1880; his library and papers can be seen to this day (fig. 91). Not far from the castle is the « Cantina » where the wines of Brolio are produced.

In the CHAPEL, built in 1348 there are some 14th. century works of art by Segna di Bonaventura and other artists of the Sienese school. The CRYPT is still the burial place of the members of the Ricasoli family. Behind the Chapel stands the castle tower, and all around, the walls which are 450 metres long. In the dining room of the modern part of the building there are some interesting Flemish tapestries and armours. See Bettino Ricasoli's apartment.

RAPOLANO TERME - Is at 30 km. from Porta Pispini, Siena (see page 153). The Whole region is rich in travertine and thermo-sulphureous water at 40° of temperature. These waters are highly recommended for baths and mud baths owing to the high percentages of carbonic anhy-

Fig. 91 - Gaiole in Chianti (surroundings) - The Castle of Brolio.

dride, sulphureous acids and bicarbonate they contain: *Bagni di San Giovanni* (temperature of the water 40°); *Bagno Antica Querciolaia* (40°) recommended for the treatment of skin diseases, rheumatism, arthritis and uricemia; *Bagni freddi di Armaiolo* (28°) for nervous complaints and enteritis. The *Stabilimento di San Giacomo a Pelacane* (36°) is recommended for the purgative properties of the water.

In the little CHIESA DELLA FRATERNITÀ, see the fragment of the many-panelled picture belonging to the school of Pietro Lorenzetti, the 16th. century fresco and Ventura Salimbeni's picture.

At 2 km. from here is SERRE DI RAPOLANO the 15th. century village which is the centre of the travertine industry. Remark the old fortress.

SINALUNGA - At 18 km. from Rapolano Terme (see above) in a delightful position 365 m. above sea level. It was once called Asinalunga (the long donkey) and was a feud of Galeazzo Visconti's who had the fortress built. In 1867 Giuseppe Garibaldi was kept a prisoner there while he was marching towards Rome. Later on the fortress was demolished and the Parish Church was built with the same old stones.

In the PARISH CHURCH (Collegiata) see the 16th. century wooden Crucifix, the panel by Girolamo del Pacchia and a lunette ascribed to Pseudo Pier Francesco Fiorentino. In the little 18th. century CHURCH OF SANTA CROCE there is an interesting painting of the school of Luca Signorelli. In the CHURCH OF THE MADONNA DELLE NEVI (of the snow), also of the 18 century, see the delightful Madonna by Benvenuto di Giovanni. In the CHAPEL OF THE SACRO CHIODO (the sacred nail) some spoilt 14th. century frescoes. In the CHURCH OF SANTA LUCIA there is another panel by Benvenuto di Giovanni and also a fresco; remark the 16th. century painted bier-heads.

TORRITA DI SIENA - At 6 km. from Sinalunga (see above) 325 m. above sea level is supposed to be the birthplace of Ghino di Tacco, the gentleman-rescal mentioned by Dante Alighieri in the VI Canto of his « *Purgatory* ». The old walls and 16th. century palaces are interesting.

In the PIEVE (*Church*) OF SANTA FIORA AND SANTA LUCILLA, a 14th. century building, there is a triptych of the Floren-

Fig 92 - Rosia (surroundings). The Cloister of the Abbey of Torri.

tine school and some of Bartolo di Fredi's and Benvenuto di Giovanni's paintings. In the ORATORY OF THE MADONNA DELLE NEVI (of the snow) see the frescoes by Benvenuto di Giovanni.

BADIA DI PONTE ALLO SPINO - otherwise Pieve di San Giovanni Battista. At 12 km. from Porta San Marco, Siena (see page 130). The Abbey is a very interesting romanesque building. The steeple has rows of windows and biforas. Inside there are three aisles and three semi-circuar apses. The pillars have fine sculptured capitals. Nearby is the ex-convent with a ruined cloister.

ROSIA - At 15 km. from Porta San Marco, Siena (see page 130) and 3 from Ponte allo Spino (see above). The pleasant little village is gathered around a characteristic romanesque Church (Pieve) with a square steeple of the Lombard kind.

In the PIEVE see the Baptismal font produced in 1332 by some artist of the school of Niccolò and Giovanni Pisano, and the panel painted by Guidoccio Cozzarelli.

At 2 km. from the Pieve there is the little mediaeval village of TORRI (253 m. above sea level) with the Abbey known as ABBAZIA VALLOMBROSIANA DI SANTA MUSTIOLA, an 11th. century building with a square cloister and three superimposed loggias, the first of which is made of black and white marble (see fig. 92). The romanesque gothic CHURCH has a very fine portal. See the panel painted by Luca di Tommè.

SAN GALGANO - At about 35 km. from Porta San Marco, Siena (see page 130) and 17 km. from Rosia (see above). It is a Cistercian Abbey built in 1324 which holds a very important place in the art and history of Siena. From 1257 to 1375 the « Camerlenghi » (Comunal administratory) of Siena were chosen from the monks of this Abbey and from 1258 to 1285 even the chief Architets for the Cathedral (called Operai del Duomo). It stood near the hill of Montesiepi where Cavalier Galgano Guidotti from Chiusdino lived a life of penitence from 1148 to 1181; a circular romanesque chapel with a hemispherical vault was built on the spot in remembrance (12th. century) decorated with frescoes of the 14th. century Sienese school. The Monastery began to decline during the 15th. century when it was deprived of the title of Abbey (1503). The vaults and the steeple fell to the ground in 1786 and the ruins are still now to be seen in all their suggestive beauty (fig. 93). The Church was never rebuilt; it has the shape of a Latin cross 69 m. long, with a nave and lateral aisles, pointed arches, ribbed vaults and pillars with sculptured capitals.

In the adjoining MONASTERY see the CHAPTER HALL.; the portal is ogival and the hall is divided into two naves by rows of pillars. The REFECTORY, too, is divided into two naves with well preserved vaults. The Friars' cells and the Chancel are also well preserved. Between the ruined Basilica and the Monastery there is still a part of the old CLOISTER wtih its pretty arches resting on double pillars.

CHIUSDINO - At 14 km. from San Galgano (see above). It is a little village lying at 564 m. above sea level within its 14th.-15th. century walls. It enjoys the view of the Merse valley (Val di Merse). Cavalier Galgano Guidotti was born here (the hermit who became San Galgano).

In the CHURCH OF THE COMPAGNIA DI SAN GALGANO there is a bas-relief of the Saint made in 1466 and some 15th. century stained glasses. In the CHURCH OF SAN MARTINO see the copper Byzantine Crucifix.

MONTICIANO - At 10 km. from Chiusdino (see above). The original nucleus of this village is still to be seen within its ancient walls.

In the CONVENT OF SANT'AGOSTINO see the frescoes painted by Bartolo di Fredi, Guidoccio Cozzarelli and Giovanni di Paolo.

Fig. 93 - Chiusdino (surroundings). The ruins of the Temple of San Galgano.

List of the illustrations

Colour Plates

Places in the province of Siena

Index

— 218 —

List of the artists

A

Ademollo Luigi (1764-1839), 136.

Agnolo di Ventura (... 1290-1349 ...), 39, 65, 68, 126, 150.

Agostino del Rosso (...1325-1349...), 39

Agostino di Agnolo (...1320-1338...), 136

Agostino di Giovanni (...1290-1350...), 38, 39, 42, 65, 68.

Albertinelli Mariotto (1474-1515), 120.

Aldi Pietro (1852-1888), 54, 158.

Ambrogio di Baldese (1352-1429), 90, 93.

Ambron Emilio (1905-v.), 59

Andrea del Sarto (1486-1541), 87.

Andrea di Bartolo (...1389-1428), 23, 110, 112.

Andrea di Niccolò (1450?-1529), 89, 116, 118

Anselmi Michelangelo (1491-1554), 120, 172.

Antiveduto della Grammatica (...1570-1626), 120.

Antonio da Sangallo il Giovane (1445-1516), 171, 175, 184, 198.

Antonio da Sangallo il Vecchio (1455-1534), 167, 186, 199.

Antonio Veneziano (...1369-1388), 44, 112.

Arnolfo di Cambio (1232-1300), 76, 87, 175, 186, 188.

Arrighetti Domenico: see Cavedone.

B

Baccio da Montelupo (1469-1535), 186.

Balducci Matteo (...1509-1555), 92, 96, 118, 152.

Balestra Pietro (...1683-1711), 83

Barbatelli Bernardino: see Poccetti Bernardino.

Barbieri Giovanni Francesco: see Guercino.

Bardi Donato di Niccolò: see Donatello.

Barili Antonio (1453-1516?), 25, 80, 84, 102, 195.

Barili Giovanni (...1505-1536...), 80.

Barili Sallustio (...1469-1490), 83.

Barna (...1340-1381), 22, 187, 188, 205.

Barna di Turino (...1379-1410...), 54.

Barozzi Jacopo: see Vignola.

Bartolo di Fredi (1330-1410), 23, 109, 110, 184, 189, 193, 196, 198, 208, 210.

Bartolomeo di Mariano (...1450-?), 99.

Bartolomeo di Tommè (...1378-1404), 25, 40.

Bartolomeo da Cortona (...1430-1462...), 87.

Bastiano del Corso (...1420-1454...), 99.

Bastiano di Francesco (...1440-1494), 70, 72, 75.

Battista di Niccolò da Padova (...1425-1438...), 39.

Bazzani Giuseppe (...1630-1665...) 118.

J

Jacopo della Quercia (1372-1438), 20, 38, 52, 54, 59, 85, 99, 100, 125, 140, 145.

Jacopo di Mino del Pellicciaio 1330-1410), 23, 99, 109, 149, 201.

L

Lambertini: see Michele di Matteo da Bologna.

Lanci Baldassarre (1510-1571), 167, 200.

Lando di Pietro (...1311-1340), 18, 25, 63, 177.

Lando di Stefano (...1355-1412...), 40.

Lapo Ciuccio di Ciuto (...1250-1269...), 76.

Lappoli Giovanni Antonio (1492-1552), 120.

Liberale da Verona (1452?-1475), 84.

Lippi Filippino (1457-1504), 189.

Lorenzetti Ambrogio (...1318-1348), 10, 22, 23, 25, 44, 49, 50, 52, 55, 92, 106, 107, 108, 109, 110, 113, 124, 125, 129, **139, 144.**

Lorenzetti Pietro (1280-1348?), 10, 22, 23, 25, 96, 106, 108, **109, 110, 138, 148, 149, 164, 196, 205.**

Lorenzetti Ugolino: see Maestro di S. Pietro a Ovile.

Lorenzo di Bartolomeo da Lucca (...1510-1550...), 80.

Lorenzo di Bicci (...1370-1427), 182.

Lorenzo di Credi (...1456-1537), 59.

Lorenzo di Mariano: see Marrina.

Lorenzo di Nicolò (...1392-1411...), 200.

Lorenzo di Pietro: see Vecchietta.

Lorenzo di Turino (...1429-?), 43.

Lorenzo Monaco (1370?-1422?), 112.

Lotto Lorenzo (1480-1556), 123.

Luca di Bartolo da Bagnacavallo (1403?-1459...), 59, 60.

Luca di Tommè (...1356-1389), 23, 110, 140.

Luciani Sebastiano: see Sebastiano del Piombo.

M

Maccari Cesare (1840-1919), 24, 54, 59, 83, 135.

Maccari Leopoldo (...1850-1891...), 67.

Maestro del Codice di S. Giorgio (14th. c.), **25.**

Maestro della Madonna di Palazzo Venezia (14th. c.), 110.

Maestro della Maestà di Londra (14th. c.), 110.

Maestro dell'Osservanza (14th. c.), 113, 176, 205.

Maestro della Vita di Maria (15th. c.), **112.**

Maestro di Badìa a Isola (14th. c.), **183.**

Maestro di Chianciano (16th. c.), 110, **200.**

Maestro di Città di Castello (14th. c.), 92, **110.**

Maestro di S. Lucchese (14th. c.), **109.**

Maestro di S. Paolo (14th. c.), 110, 200.

Maestro di S. Pietro a Ovile (14th. c.), 109, 141.

Maffei Francesco (...1625-1660...), 118.

Magagni Girolamo: see Giomo del Sodoma.

Magi Giovanni (...1852-1895...), 54.

Mainardi Sebastiano (1450-1513), 187, 189.

Maitani Gano (...1282-1310...), 20.

Maitani Lorenzo (1275?-1330), 20.

Piero della Francesca (1416-1492), 118.

Pietro del Minella (1391-1458), 20, 70, 72, 78, 99.

Pietro di Domenico (1457-1503?), 116, 117, 189.

Pietro di Francesco degli Orioli (...1458-1496...), 99.

Pietro di Giovanni di Ambrogio (1410-1449), 113, 176, 205.

Pinturicchio (1454-1518), 23, 59, 70, 81, 83, 84, 87, 100, 118, 171, 178, 189.

Pisano Giovanni (1248?-1319?), 20, 43, 62, 64, 65, 76, 77, 86, 87, 90, 96, 138.

Pisano Nicola (1206-1280), 20, 62, 75, 76, 87.

Poccetti Bernardino (1548-1612), 102, 123, 178.

Pollaiolo Piero (del) (1443-1496), 23, 187.

Pomarancio (Il) (1552-1626), 87, 88, 122, 157, 158.

Ponsi Domenico (...1498-1507...), 97.

Pontormo Jacopo (1494-1556), 59.

Porrina Pietro Paolo (del) (...1460-1472...), 143.

Posi Paolo (1708-1776), 137.

Pozzo Andrea del (1642-1709), 198.

Preti Mattia (1613-1699), 78, 143, 164.

Preziani Ottavio (1550?-1603...), 129.

Priamo della Quercia (...1432-1467...), 94.

Prospero da Brescia (...1579-1592?), 150.

Prunai Arnoldo (1846-1917), 54.

Q

Quaroni Giorgio (1907-1960), 163.

Quercia: see Jacopo e Priamo della

R

Raffaello (1483-1520), 24.

Raffaello da Brescia (Fra) (1479-1539), 191.

Raggi Antonio (1624-1686), 77, 78.

Ramo di Paganello (...1281-1314), 20, 64.

Redi Tommaso (1602-1657), 65, 68.

Reni Guido (1574-1642), 145.

Repossi Pietro (1897-liv.), 160.

Riccio (1520-1573?), 43, 47, 75, 78, 80, 88, 96, 120, 135, 157, 176, 199.

Robbia Ambrogio della (...1509-?), 151.

Robbia Andrea della (1437-1528), 176, 199.

Robbia Luca della (1400-1482), 195, 199.

Romanelli Giovanni Francesco 1610?-1662), 126, 167.

Romanelli Raffaello (1856-1928), 144, 174.

Roncalli Cristoforo: see Pomarancio.

Rosa Salvator (1615-1673), 59.

Rosselli Cosimo (1439-1507), 118.

Rossellino Bernardo (1409-1464), 19, 53, 59, 143, 183, 197.

Rossi Giulio (...1848-1854...), 60, 101.

Rosso: see Giuseppe del Rosso.

Rubens Pierre Paul (1577-1640), 122.

Rustichino (Il) (1595-1625), 59, 83, 84, 96, 124, 146, 171.

Rustici Cristoforo: see Rusticone.

Rustici Francesco: see Rustichino.

Rustici Lorenzo: see Rustico.

Rustico (Il) (1521-1572), 56, 135.

Rusticone (Il) (1550-1640), 149.